Better Homes and Gardens®

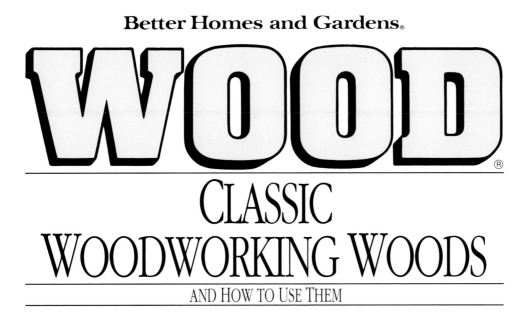

WOOD®

CLASSIC
WOODWORKING WOODS

AND HOW TO USE THEM

A **WOOD**® **BOOK**
Published by Meredith® Books

MEREDITH® BOOKS
President, Book Group: Joseph J. Ward
Vice President and Editorial Director: Elizabeth P. Rice
Executive Editor: Connie Schrader
Art Director: Ernest Shelton
Prepress Production Manager: Randall Yontz

WOOD® MAGAZINE
President, Magazine Group: William T. Kerr
Editor: Larry Clayton

CLASSIC WOODWORKING WOODS AND HOW TO USE THEM
Produced by Roundtable Press, Inc.
Directors: Susan E. Meyer, Marsha Melnick
Senior Editor: Marisa Bulzone
Managing Editor: Ross L. Horowitz
Graphic Designer: Leah Lococo
Design Assistant: Betty Lew
Art Assistant: Mariana Canelo Francis
Proofreader: Amy Handy

For Meredith® Books
Editorial Project Manager/Associate Art Director: Tom Wegner
Contributing Editor: Peter J. Stephano
Contributing Techniques Editor: Bill Krier
Contributing Outline Editor: David A. Kirchner

Special thanks to Khristy Benoit

Meredith Corporation Corporate Officers:
Chairman of the Executive Committee: E. T. Meredith III
Chairman of the Board, President and Chief Executive Officer:
    Jack D. Rehm
Group Presidents: Joseph J. Ward, Books; William T. Kerr, Magazines;
    Philip A. Jones, Broadcasting; Allen L. Sabbag, Real Estate
Vice Presidents: Leo R. Armatis, Corporate Relations;
    Thomas G. Fisher, General Counsel and Secretary;
    Larry D. Hartsook, Finance; Michael A. Sell, Treasurer;
    Kathleen J. Zehr, Controller and Assistant Secretary

WOOD 101: BASICS YOU SHOULD KNOW

In this complete primer we tell you how to pick the choicest cuts of wood for all your projects. From the principles of buymanship to wood properties and terminology, you'll gain the knowledge needed to be well prepared for a trip to the lumberyard.

NINE QUESTIONS WOODWORKERS ASK ABOUT HARDWOOD

If you think you're the only one who has questions about buying hardwoods, think again! We surveyed eight hardwood dealers from around the country—perhaps one of these guys sold you a piece of wood last week—and here's what they hear from customers day after day.

1. What do flat-, rift-, and quarter-sawed mean?

Some mill operators try to squeeze as much usable lumber as possible out of a log, so they run the raw stock through a blade that slices off one board after another.

This through-and-through cutting method creates about 80 percent flat-sawed lumber. A log can be cut to yield a lower percentage of flat-sawed lumber, but with considerably greater time, effort, and wastage. Here's a brief guide to the three types of sawed lumber:

Flat-sawed: As shown *below*, grain patterns run in long, sweeping lines almost parallel to the face of the board, creating the familiar cathedral face figure. According to Dick Boak of the Martin Guitar Company in Nazareth, Pennsylvania, these boards have a greater tendency to cup, twist, or crack (especially near the middle of the board) than lumber in the next two categories.

Rift-sawed: Grain lines run at about 45° to the face of the board. In some species, these boards show a beautiful figure in the form of long, sweeping stripes resulting from the rays that run from the center of the tree toward the bark. You'll often see this figure in oak.

Quarter-sawed: With grain lines running at 90° to the face, these cuts produce strong, stable boards with straight-grain face figure. Manufacturers of products that require strong woods, such as cue-stick makers, purchase large quantities of quarter-sawed lumber. For example, Howard Hughes built his infamous *Spruce Goose* almost entirely of "aircraft-quality" or quarter-sawed spruce. You can specify quarter-sawed boards from some producers, but expect to pay a premium price.

2. I'm making a gift for a woman. What woods should I use? What woods appeal more to men?

"Women prefer light-colored woods and woods with more 'flash,' such as Brazilian tulipwood, bird's-eye maple, purpleheart, and Brazilian satinwood," according to Jim Huesinger of Berea Hardwoods of Berea, Ohio. How does Huesinger know this? "When a man and woman shop for wood together, I often hear the woman say 'Look at this beautiful wood!' And that is usually the wood they buy."

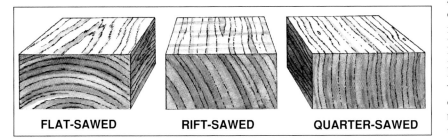

FLAT-SAWED   RIFT-SAWED   QUARTER-SAWED

continued

NINE QUESTIONS WOODWORKERS ASK ABOUT HARDWOOD
continued

"On the other hand, men seem to prefer dark, rich woods with straighter grain, such as walnut, wenge, bubinga, ebony, cocobolo, and mahogany."

3. What does "random width and length" mean, and why can't I buy hardwoods in dimensional sizes (1×6, 2×4, 2×8, etc.)?

"Because hardwood trees take longer to grow—making them more valuable than softwoods—they're cut in random widths and lengths to yield as much wood as possible from each log," says Dave Forness of Northeastern Hardwoods in Salamanca, New York. "Loggers die bringing these hardwoods out of the forest, so I hate to see anything wasted. On the other hand, relatively inexpensive softwood logs are cut to the standard sizes necessary in the building trades, leaving a lot of waste on the floor of the mill."

But consumer demand changes the market. Some hardwood outlets, including Frank Paxton Beautiful Wood stores in the central part of the country, now sell some hardwoods in dimensional sizes.

"Five years ago, you couldn't have sold hardwoods that way, but people don't seem to mind paying the extra price for it," says Bob Byers of Paxton's Denver store. For example, red oak finished on three sides (both faces and

straightline ripped on one edge) sells for $3.69 per board foot in random widths and lengths at Paxton's. The same species finished on four sides, in 1×12 dimension, sells for $5.05 per lineal foot—a cost difference of about 36 percent.

Officials at Weyerhaeuser Corporation in Titusville, Pennsylvania, seem to agree with Byers' assessment, because the firm now markets dimensioned hardwoods in 3,600 home centers and hardware stores nationwide. Through its Choice-woods program, the company surfaces hardwood on four sides and sells it in 2"–8" widths, in 3'–8' lengths, and in red oak, poplar, maple, cherry, walnut, western red alder, and ash. For this highly finished product, you'll pay a premium price. For example, a 1"×6"×6' red oak board costs $16.99, or $5.66 per board foot.

Why? "We guarantee every board to be free of defects, so we only get a 42 percent yield from each log," says Doug Bolton of Weyerhaeuser.

4. What woods are toxic?

"I wouldn't sell any wood if it was poisonous—that would be insane," Jim Huesinger says about so-called toxic woods. "Some woods, such as cocobolo or Western red cedar, cause more allergic reactions than other woods, but sensitivity to all woods varies greatly from individual to individual. My advice: If you notice a reaction such as a rash when you're working around a specific wood, just stop using that

wood. And since wood dust of any type can harm you, it only makes sense to wear a dust mask no matter what wood you're working. Also wash frequently and use a barrier cream on hands and face!"

For more information , see "What You should Know About Toxic Wood" on *page 21*.

5. What does 4/4 (pronounced "4 quarter"), 5/4, etc. mean?

Dick D'Abate of Woodworkers Supply in Phoenix, Arizona, hears this question often, and here's how he answers it: "A board that's 7/4 started as a 1¾"-thick board and was surfaced on both sides and is now 1½"-thick. An 8/4 board was 2" thick in its rough state and ⅛" was surfaced off both sides to make it a 1¾" board, and so on. We carry up to 16/4 boards (4" boards surfaced to a thickness of 3¾")."

According to National Hardwood Lumber Association (NHLA) specifications, the idea that dressed boards are always ¼" less thick than their unsurfaced thickness works only for 7/4 and thicker boards. For instance, a 6/4 board can be surfaced to a minimum of 1⁵⁄₁₆" thickness, a 5/4 board must be at least 1¹⁄₁₆" thick after dressing, and a 4/4 board cannot be surfaced to less than ¹³⁄₁₆".

Because few mills cut hardwood lumber less than 4/4 thick, you will pay the price of 4/4 stock, plus surfacing charges, for any board ¹³⁄₁₆" thick and less. As Bob Garst, assistant manager of the NHLA puts it: "When you buy wood, you're buying two things: the wood and the modification to that wood."

6. I'm just getting started in woodworking; what are some good but inexpensive woods to work with?

"When I feel a woodworker doesn't have the necessary equipment or expertise for a given project, I steer him toward yellow poplar at about $1.25 per board foot, or knotty white pine at about $1 per board foot," says Bob Carr of Educational Lumber Co. in Asheville, North Carolina. "Both of these woods work well and have good strength, and yellow poplar is fairly stable. Neither will break most pocketbooks if a project doesn't work out the first time."

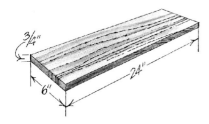

7. How do I calculate board footage?

Some woodworkers order their wood by the board foot and others simply take a cutting diagram to their supplier. In any case, the hardwood outlet will charge you by board footage, so it helps to know how to figure it out.

"I get this question fairly often," said Dick D'Abate, "and the answer is pretty simple. First, you take the thickness of the board before the board was surfaced (1" for a 4/4 board), multiply that figure times length in inches, then multiply that figure times width in inches, and divide by 144. For instance, a ¾" board that's 6" wide and 2' long started as a 1"-thick board so the equation goes: 1"x 6"x24" equals 144; divide 144 by 144 and you have one board foot."

8. What woods are waterproof?

For outdoor projects, Dick Boak recommends these woods: western red cedar, true mahoganies, redwood, and teak. Avoid lauan—it lacks the water-repelling tight grain of true mahoganies.

9. How is lumber graded?

Most hardwood outlets that cater to the home woodworker sell only firsts and seconds (usually combined as one grade called FAS)—the highest grade for hardwood lumber. In the FAS grade, boards will yield a minimum of 83⅓ percent clear cuttings at least 3"x7' or 4"x5'. Common uses for these boards include quality furniture, interior trim, and solid wood moldings.

In the next grade down, Selects, one face is FAS, the other is No. 1 common.

No. 1 common boards will yield from 66⅔ to 83⅓ percent clear wood cuttings at least 3"x3' or 4"x2'. They are best suited for furniture and cabinets.

No. 2 common boards find use as unexposed furniture components, and picture and cabinet frames. The boards will yield 50 to 66⅔ percent clear wood cuttings at least 3"x2' in size.

For more information, send $1.50 ppd. for *An Introduction to Grading Hardwood Lumber*, from the National Hardwood Lumber Association, P.O. Box 34518, Memphis, TN 38184.

WHAT YOU NEED TO KNOW ABOUT BUYING BOARDS

A project that draws applause begins with stable, good-looking stock. But selecting and buying hardwood by grade and board feet puzzles many home woodworkers. And overlooked defects can prove disastrous. Here's how to make shopping easier.

Ken Palmer, of Londonderry, New Hampshire, an airline pilot and *WOOD®* magazine reader, builds fine furniture in his off-hours. He wrote to Paul McClure, our wood technology consultant:

"I recently purchased 170 leftover red oak boards at 70 cents per board foot from a casket company. After I had it planed, the wood looked aged and seemed brittle. When I started working it, the boards split so easily that I could snap them along the grain like scored glass. What's wrong with my wood?"

According to Paul, Ken's bargain red oak boards suffer from collapse. That's the term for a distortion and deterioration of the cell walls that happens when wood with a high moisture content—especially red oak—dries too rapidly. Unfortunately, this condition makes Ken's purchase only good for firewood.

Because most of you buy stock from established, reliable sources, you might think that situations like Ken's rarely occur. But in truth, you can buy a bad board anywhere. That's why we searched out some expert help to lead us down the potentially splinter-filled path of buying hardwood by the board.

Showing tips from the pros

To help you avoid disappointments, we first contacted Jim Huesinger, owner of Berea Hardwoods in Berea, Ohio. He gave us some practical, common-sense shopping suggestions.

"First, just how do you know if the wood is dry? You have to ask, test the wood with a moisture meter, or feel it," says the hardwood expert. "But you don't really need a moisture meter. If the weather is relatively warm, put your upper lip against it. A cold surface indicates that the wood isn't dry. Kiln-dried wood at 9 percent or less has a warm feeling."

When you're convinced of the wood's dryness, start looking for your project boards. Jim follows a regular procedure. "I sort through and find those that will work and those that definitely won't," he says. "The boards must have the right color, with no or few appearance defects, straight grain, no warp or twist, no collapse, and no sloping grain [runoff].

"To make sure there's no cupping or twist, I put each board on the floor and turn it over to see if it lays flat. I've even been known to bring along a crayon to mark the ones I want."

Dave Boykin, a professional furnituremaker and designer in Denver, Colorado, adds some advice. "I buy boards by size in terms of the cuttings I need, color, and grain," he says. "And that's especially tough when you deal with unsurfaced stock, because you can't see the wood's true color and grain."

To assist his decision making, Dave carries a little pocketknife with him to the lumberyard. "I scrape the surface clear in an area on one end of the board, and at a spot on the edge," he notes.

Dave also cautions about moisture content. "If you have any doubt about dryness, ask to borrow a moisture meter. Any reputable dealer has one handy, and will loan it to you. I check every board that I use."

How much wood do you need for your project?

When you build from a project plan, such as the ones we provide in *WOOD®* magazine, list your lumber needs as described in the bill of materials and cutting diagram. Knowing the size and number of boards you must buy, and the cuttings you'll get from them, happens to be far more important than trying to figure your needs in board feet, the hardwood lumber industry's standard unit of measurement and sale. (For an explanation of board feet, see the box, *opposite.)*

"Then, don't forget to allow about 20 percent for waste, even in the top grades of FAS and Select," advises the Ohio expert. "If you plan to buy lower grade, No. 1 Common boards, allow more."

Although Jim uses the terms FAS, Select, and No. 1 Common, he admits that exactly understanding their meaning isn't mandatory for a hobbyist, unless you shop by mail or otherwise sight unseen (see the box, *right*, for grades). "Instead, focus on what you expect the wood to be, and then look for it," Jim says.

"You have to ask for what you want in plain English," Jim continues. "To use cherry as an example, if you want the unfinished wood to be all orange-brown, without any lighter sapwood showing, say so. Then, you'll be pointed in the right direction. Will you accept sapwood or knots on the back of the boards, where they won't show in the project? To the dealer, that means a less costly grade than if you said, 'I only want all-clear wood.' "

Jim agrees with the Denver woodworker about the possible dangers of buying unsurfaced lumber—advice that might have served Ken Palmer well. "Let's say you're looking at unsurfaced lumber that you're told is Select grade," he says. "That means that only one side has to be FAS—the other side can be No. 1 Common. What are you going to do when you get those boards home and plane them down to $^{13}/_{16}$" or whatever, and the wood you take off the FAS face reveals the defects of the poorer side?"

"And finally," says Dave Boykin, "you can't forget about moisture content after you get your wood home. All wood should acclimate to the relative humidity where it will be used once made into a project. So, sticker your wood for a week or so in your house—or the shop, if it's the same humidity level as your home. You can also stand it straight up on end. With thick pieces, saw the boards into the approximate cutting sizes you need. That helps it acclimate to your home faster."

What you get from a grade

Generally, the hardwood boards you'll buy fall into the three top grades as established by the National Hardwood Lumber Association, and as explained and illustrated *below*.

First and Seconds (FAS): This grade yields the most clear wood from the widest and longest boards.

Selects: This provides the same amount of clear wood as FAS, but it comes from only one side of narrower and shorter boards. The back side has defects as found in the next lower grade.

No. 1 Common: An economical grade for uses requiring short and narrow clear cuts. This grade has about one-third waste.

Splits

Splits

Split

Shaded area equals clear cuttings

Understanding hardwood measure

Hardwood lumber thickness is expressed in quarters of an inch instead of inches and fractions. Four-quarter (4/4) equals 1"-thick stock, 6/4 adds up to 1½" material, and so on. This applies to unsurfaced stock. Wood surfaced four sides (S4S) and surfaced two sides (S2S) measures about ⅛" thinner than rough stock. Hardwood boards also come in random widths and lengths rather than standard thicknesses and widths (1×6, 2×4, etc.), because mills saw for clearest yield with the least amount of waste. Too, you buy hardwood by the board foot, a unit that equals 144 cubic inches of wood, instead of the running foot. Think of a board foot as a piece of stock 1" thick and 12" square.

Dealers figure board footage in quarters of an inch thickness, starting at 1" (even if you order less). So, a 5/4 board 6" wide and 72" long represents 3.75 board feet. Here's the calculation: 1.25 (thickness)×6 (width) ×72 (length) equals 540 cubic inches. Divide 540 by 144 to determine the number of board feet in the stock (3.75).

CHOOSING AND BUYING CABINET-QUALITY LUMBER

The wood used for furniture and other fine projects differs in many ways from lumberyard 2x4s. Here's where you find out how and why.

Long-time woodworkers have learned through experience the importance of choosing their lumber carefully. They know which species perform well in certain situations, which thicknesses are needed for various projects, and dozens of other important things about choosing and using this most intriguing material. This article attempts to share some of that hard-won knowledge with you.

The first thing to realize about cabinet-quality lumber is that the rules you probably know about ordering dimension lumber (the type you use for carpentry work) don't apply. Sizing, grading, ordering—they're all different.

Also keep in mind that except for a few white pines, such as Sugar and Idaho, redwood, and aromatic cedar, most of the time you'll be working with hardwoods. (See the list of popular lumber species *below*.)

Understanding moisture content

All cabinet-grade lumber begins as a "green" board that's been mill-sawed from a freshly felled tree. The moisture content of a green board will be 28 percent or greater, making it unsuitable for woodworking, since all wood shrinks, warps, and splits as it dries.

To remove moisture from green boards, most manufacturers air-dry and kiln-dry them. Air-drying reduces the moisture content naturally—workers stack the slabs in such a way that air circulates between the separated layers of boards. Air-drying lowers the

moisture level to between 12 and 17 percent. (This is acceptable for outdoor construction, but don't make any interior projects using air-dried material.)

Kiln-drying takes over where air-drying leaves off. Large oven-like kilns with carefully controlled temperatures reduce the moisture content to between 6 and 9 percent, the ideal range for interior projects.

With few exceptions, such as dense woods like ebony, which usually are air-dried, retail hardwood dealers sell only kiln-dried lumber. It's stored, and sold, indoors under a roof where the elements won't affect it.

When you purchase kiln-dried lumber, store it indoors lying flat on dry sticks of scrap or hardboard. Never lay it directly on concrete because it will absorb excessive moisture. If left exposed to the elements outdoors, kiln-dried lumber can become useless for fine cabinetry. In most cases, though, moisture absorbed will be of the surface type, and the boards will return to their former dryness after storage time in the shop.

How cabinet-grade lumber is sized

Unlike dimension lumber, which is milled to industry-established nominal thicknesses, widths, and lengths, most cabinet-quality stock comes in random widths and lengths to keep waste to an absolute minimum. In addition, since all furniture has different dimensions, there's no need for dimensionalized stock.

Thickness, though, has been standardized. As you can see from the chart *opposite top*, thickness is expressed in different ways. Don't be confused by this; remember that the quarter

Commonly Used Species		
Species	**Characteristics**	**Relative Cost**
Ash (White)	Broad grain pattern, strong, easy to bend, easy to work, tends to split.	Moderate
Birch	Finishes well, can be made to resemble more expensive woods.	Moderate
Cherry	Machines and finishes well, though it has a tendency to burn when sawed or routed.	Moderate
Genuine Mahogany	Works and finishes well, relatively easy to work.	Moderate
Philippine Mahogany (Red Lauan)	Easy to work, coarse texture, finishes well.	Inexpensive
Maple (Hard)	Most adaptable of all hardwoods, takes stain and works well.	Moderate
Oak (Red & White)	Strong, heavy, finishes well, difficult to shape.	Moderate
Pine (Sugar, Eastern, Idaho)	Finishes well, easy to work.	Expensive (Clear Grades)
Poplar	Moderately easy to work, finishes well, fairly weak, doesn't hold nails well.	Inexpensive
Redwood	Easy to work, lightweight, finishes well.	Varies By Grade
Walnut	Strong, durable, works and finishes well, fine grain.	Expensive

STANDARDIZED LUMBER THICKNESSES AND USES

Quarter Designation	Thickness			Uses
	Nominal	Actual	Pine	
5/8	⅝" material	½" or ⁷⁄₁₆"	same	Laminating, drawer sides and backs
4/4	1" material	²⁵⁄₃₂" or ¾"	same	Majority of work, face frames, shelves, and making up sides for width, jigs
5/4	1¼" material	1¹⁄₁₆"	1⁵⁄₃₂"	Table and other tops, furniture parts
6/4	1½" material	1⁵⁄₁₆"	1¹³⁄₃₂"	Moldings, leg to rail construction and bases
8/4	2" material	1¾"	1¹³⁄₁₆"	Framing members, table legs, workbenches, turning

designation and the nominal thickness are the same animal.

When you order cabinet-quality lumber, you'll receive a board as long as or longer than and as wide as or wider than the item ordered. The thickness (if surfaced) will be close to that listed in the chart.

Buying by the board foot

Until the late 1800s, lumber was sold by the pound. Under that system, dry boards were less expensive than green wood. So obviously something had to be done.

The system of measurement that evolved centers around the *board foot,* a measurement that covers all the dimensional variables of cabinet-grade lumber—thickness, width, and length.

Today, when you purchase this type of lumber, you buy it by the board foot. Even if the dealer has the boards already priced, he arrived at those prices by first figuring the number of board feet each contained. It's a good practice to double-check the dealer's figures. To do this and also to help

you estimate your lumber needs, you should learn how to figure board feet .

A board foot, simply, is equal to 144 cubic inches of wood. Think of it as a piece 1 inch thick and 12 inches square. Since board footage is always calculated in quarters of an inch thickness, starting at no less than 1 inch (even if you order less than an inch, you'll pay for the 1-inch thickness), a 5/4 board 6 inches wide and 72 inches long would be figured like this: 1.25 (thickness)x6 (width)x72 (length)=540. Divide 540 by 144 to determine the number of board feet in the stock. If the board length is stated in feet rather than inches, use the same method but divide your total by 12 instead of 144.

How cabinet-quality lumber is graded

Unlike dimension lumber, which manufacturers grade according to its use in construction as full width and length members, hardwood is graded according to the expected number of clear face cuts a board will yield. And, since most hardwood is expected to be made into furniture, these cuts will be from 2 to 7 feet long. For more information on the hardwood grading system, which was developed by the National Hardwood Lumber Association, see the chart at *left.* This same chart also discusses the grading system for white pine, which was formulated by the Western Wood Products Association. In cabinet lumber there are great differences in quality, just as there are in construction lumber, so use the chart as a guide.

Remember, too, that in building a large project such as a table or desk top, you'll generally need the higher grades of lumber because they have fewer defects and are available in greater widths and lengths than lower-grade boards.

Many retail hardwood dealers

continued

LUMBER GRADES

Grade	Characteristics
HARDWOODS First and seconds (FAS)	The best grade. Boards usually 6" and wider, 8' and longer. Almost clear. Yields 83⅓ percent of clear face cuttings 4" or wider by 5' or longer and 3" or wider by 7' or longer.
Selects	Boards are 4" and wider, 6' and longer. One side is FAS, the other is No. 1 Common. Yields 83⅓ percent clear face cuttings
No. 1 Common (Thrift Grade)	Boards are 3" and wider, 4' and longer. Economical alternative for some uses. Yields 66⅔ percent of clear face cuttings 4" or wider by 2' or longer and 3" or wider by 3' or longer.
SOFTWOODS C Select & Better	Minor imperfections.
D Select	A few sound defects.
3rd Clear	The best shop grade. Acceptable for cabinets. Well-placed knots allow for high percentage of clear cuts.
No. 1 Shop	More knots and fewer clear cuts than 3rd Clear.
Nos. 2 and 3 Common	The so-called shelving grades. No. 2 has fewer knots that No. 3

For more information contact:
National Hardwood Lumber Association, Box 34518, Memphis TN 38134
Western Wood Products Association, 1500 Yeon Bldg., Portland, OR 97204

CHOOSING AND BUYING CABINET-QUALITY LUMBER
continued

carry only the highest grades possible to avoid customer complaints and discount requests.

Estimating your needs

Before you purchase any lumber for a project, draw a cutting diagram, and figure the board footage needed. And, if at all possible, buy from a dealer who will allow you to hand-select your boards. Hand-selecting gives you two distinct advantages. First, you can choose the grain, color, and texture you'd like to have. Second, you'll be able to select your lumber in sizes that accommodate your cutting list and thus reduce waste. If you cannot choose your own lumber, allow about 20 percent for waste and add it to your needed board footage.

Where to buy cabinet-quality lumber

In addition to the cabinet-quality lumber available from lumberyards, home centers, and retail specialty stores, you have the option of mail-order buying.

The number of firms offering quality hardwood by mail has mushroomed and you're likely to find one close to your area of the country. Most firms offer a variety of dimensions and species as well as veneers and turning blocks. Though you'll be able to order pieces down to ¼" in thickness, lengths will normally be limited to about 6 feet, since shipping traditionally is done via UPS or parcel post. You can make alternate shipping arrangements for oversize and larger amounts, but you'll have to discuss your purchase on the telephone. Discounts on large orders often apply. Some companies include shipping in their catalog prices; others charge separately.

Mail-order lumber definitely addresses a need for those woodworkers who don't have a supplier nearby. And the quality will be the highest possible for each specie offered.

If you have any questions or are uncertain of your needs before you order, call the company. That way you'll receive exactly what you require.

Note: *When ordering by mail from an area of different climate, such as Pennsylvania when your home is in Arizona, keep this in mind: differences in temperature and humidity cause changes in the wood and so can adversely affect the outcome of a project if you use it right away. So be sure to allow the wood to acclimate in a dry spot in your shop for at least two weeks before working.*

One other lumber-purchasing option deserves mention because it sounds attractive to lots of people. And that alternative is green wood. In rural areas you can normally go directly to the logger and purchase a felled and delimbed log, then hew it yourself, or take it to a mill. Or you can go directly to an area sawyer for the log and for any custom-cutting you desire. In metropolitan areas, you often can find green wood for free from tree-trimming services, water works and parks departments, and county and state highway departments.

Our advice on purchasing green wood is brief and to the point: Unless you have prior experience with green wood and know how to bring its moisture content down, stick with kiln-dried material.

HOW TO BE A HARDWOOD SUPERSLEUTH

When you can't positively identify a hardwood, do like the pros—take a closer look.

We see the same question over and over in reader letters: "The wood profile in every issue sure helps to identify standing trees. But, isn't there a way to tell what the wood might be when it's down and dry or cut up in a firewood pile?"

It's probably a crying shame how much potentially good hardwood for carving, turning, and even boards has been passed by because no one knew it was worth the bother. And, there isn't a pocket-sized, field identification guide book we know about that helps you name downed logs and chunks.

Field guides seem to be published for summertime hikers. They rely on illustrations or photographs of leaves, twigs, and standing trees. That's all fine and dandy, but if all you have to look at is a chunk of wood you think might make a great bowl, no way! So, we went to the pros for help.

Search for clues

Botanist Donna Christensen solves identity mysteries every day in the wood anatomy research section of the U.S. Forest Service's Forest Products Laboratory in Madison, Wisconsin. According to her, you can name an anonymous hardwood through a number of tests (see "Tests for identifying downed timber," *page 14*). "If one test doesn't give you a clue, apply another until you find the solution," she advises.

Botanists and dendrologists (those who study trees) usually can identify a wood quickly. When they're still stumped, however, they put their eye to a microscope to check a wood sample for telltale structure. We

discovered that even amateur wood detectives can tell, at least generally (such as hickory or oak), what wood they have by looking at it the same way—close up—with the help of a hand lens.

How to recognize a wood by its parts

Hardwood species have "fingerprints." Their fingerprints are the differently structured parts and appearance of the annual growth rings (see photograph, *below*).

In some hardwoods it doesn't take magnification to see the annual growth rings in the end grain. However, it's the size of the pores or cellular structures called vessels and where they fall in both

the earlywood and the latewood that help classify and identify hardwoods with a hand lens. (See photographs and species classification on *page 15*.)

Ring-porous species display a clear distinction in size between pores in the earlywood, developed during the first part of the growing season, and those in the latewood, produced when trees grow slowly. Diffuse-porous species, on the other hand, have pores of approximately the same size distributed throughout the ring. Scientists call wood showing pores of various sizes throughout the growth ring semi-ring porous.

continued

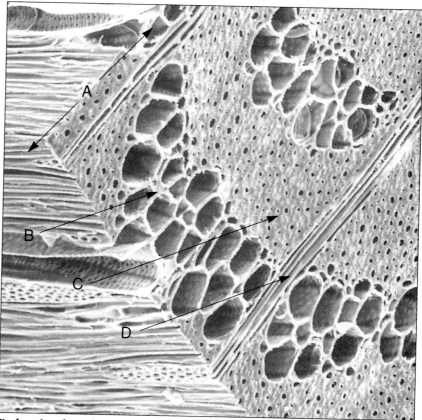

End grain of an elm tree. A: Growth ring. B: Earlywood pores. C: Latewood pores. D: Rays.

HOW TO BE A HARDWOOD SUPERSLEUTH
continued

Rays can aid you in identifying hardwoods too. Most often you'll see them as fine lines crosshatching the wood at regularly spaced intervals perpendicular to the growth rings. In the oaks, they're bold.

Put a hand lens to hardwood

To see pores and rays clearly with a hand lens, slice the end grain of your log in the heartwood with a sharp blade. Next, dampen the fresh surface slightly, then focus the lens.

The photos *opposite*, taken at hand-lens magnification, then nearly doubled in size for added clarity, show what you'll see in 15 common hardwoods. Study the end grain of other species with a hand lens. You'll build knowledge, and a Scotland Yard reputation.

References for a super sleuth

To keep you from barking up the wrong tree, we suggest:

Trees of North America, a Guide to Field Identification, by C. Frank Brockman, 1979, The Golden Press, NY (pocket-size, illustrated, easy-to-use handbook).

The Audubon Society Field Guide to North American Trees, by Elbert L. Little, 1986, Alfred A. Knopf, NY (handbook with photographs, keys to identification, east/west regional editions).

Wood Structure and Identification, by H. A. Core, W. A. Côté, A. C. Day, 1979, Syracuse University Press, Syracuse, NY.

Where you can buy a hand lens: Opticians, jewelry stores, and jewelry supply houses sell 10X magnification hand lenses for about $10.

Tests for identifying downed timber

• **Should it grow here?** A reference book can help weed out lots of trees. Little tips such as "range limited to coast of northwest Oregon" save you extended probing if the downed tree you're identifying happens to be in upstate New York.

• **Use common sense and scents.** Sheer size eliminates some candidates. It would be the rare persimmon that grew to oak-size.

Activate a wood's scent by cutting a fresh spot or chip in the heartwood, then rub in a little saliva. With many woods, an identifiable smell lingers even when it has been down a long time and is as dry as a bone. Practice sniffing the hardwoods you know when you work them in the shop.

• **Does color ring a bell?** Osage orange's bright-yellow wood pegs it right away. And who could mistake the distinctive, dark richness of black walnut? Would you recognize cherry? Study dry, unfinished stock to build up your recognition bank. On downed wood, you'll have to chip away dirty, weathered wood to see any true color.

• **Is it bogus bark?** Sometimes a good clue, as with white birch. But bark varies too much to always be reliable. Walnut sometimes has bark that resembles black cherry. Trees of varying ages in the same species can have entirely different-looking bark. Where a tree grows and the rate it grows also affect bark color and texture.

• **Work the wood.** Use a knife or a hatchet to remove a section of outer bark about the size of your shoe. Keep peeling until you've gone through the inner bark. When you get to solid wood, slice a flat surface. The color may be lighter, because you're looking at sapwood, but the grain runs the same as flat-sawn stock from your hardwood dealer.

What you see is what you get— Classifying hardwoods with a hand lens

Use the hardwoods shown below as a reference when identifying wood with a hand lens. First, decide what cell structure your wood sample has, then see if it matches any of those illustrated.

Remember, you might only be able to name the wood generally, such as *birch*. If you're still not sure of your identification, apply the test described *opposite*. Become familiar with the cell structure of known hardwoods you have in the shop and found where you live. A tree guidebook comes in handy, too.

RING-POROUS

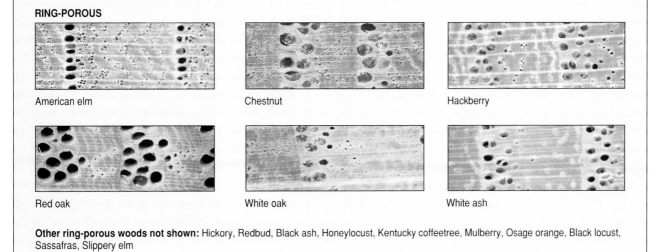

American elm

Chestnut

Hackberry

Red oak

White oak

White ash

Other ring-porous woods not shown: Hickory, Redbud, Black ash, Honeylocust, Kentucky coffeetree, Mulberry, Osage orange, Black locust, Sassafras, Slippery elm

DIFFUSE-POROUS

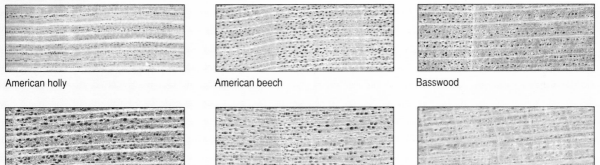

American holly

American beech

Basswood

Black cherry

Red alder

Sugar maple

Other diffuse-porous woods not shown: Red maple, Buckeye, Pacific madrone, Yellow birch, River birch, American hornbeam, Flowering dogwood, Yellow poplar, Magnolia, Tupelo gum, Eastern hophornbeam, Sourwood, Sycamore, Aspen, Cottonwood, Willow, Myrtle

SEMI-RING POROUS

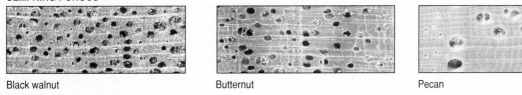

Black walnut

Butternut

Pecan

Other semi-ring porous woods not shown: Catalpa, Persimmon, Tanoak, Cascara buckthorn

.RACKING DOWN GOOD WOOD

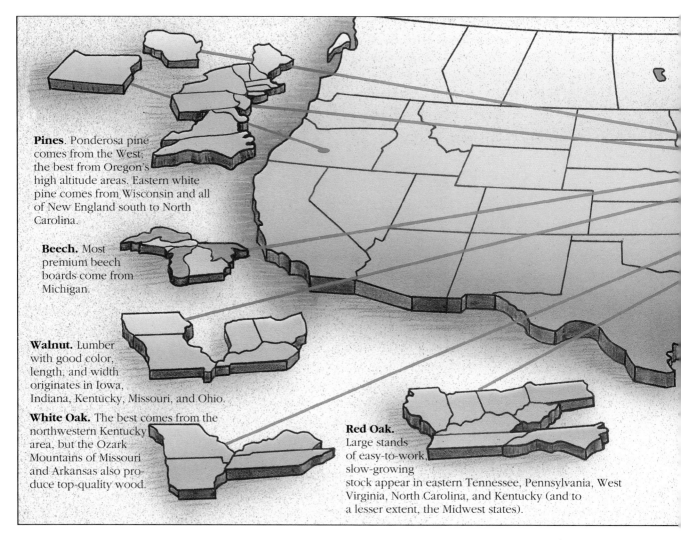

Pines. Ponderosa pine comes from the West; the best from Oregon's high altitude areas. Eastern white pine comes from Wisconsin and all of New England south to North Carolina.

Beech. Most premium beech boards come from Michigan.

Walnut. Lumber with good color, length, and width originates in Iowa, Indiana, Kentucky, Missouri, and Ohio.

White Oak. The best comes from the northwestern Kentucky area, but the Ozark Mountains of Missouri and Arkansas also produce top-quality wood.

Red Oak. Large stands of easy-to-work, slow-growing stock appear in eastern Tennessee, Pennsylvania, West Virginia, North Carolina, and Kentucky (and to a lesser extent, the Midwest states).

Wood is wood, right? Wrong! Hardwood trees with all the favored woodworking attributes of their individual species don't grow just anywhere. Neither do your favorite softwoods. Here's where professional lumber buyers seek super stock.

Have you ever wondered why one board, say of red oak, machines better than another from a batch you bought at your wood supplier? Or why a piece of ash stock you hefted in your friend's shop seemed heavier than one you have on

hand? Well, commercial hardwood buyers will tell you that the reason for the difference stems from the wood's origin. And that also holds true for softwoods.

"By and large, the majority of the best North American hardwoods are harvested from the northerly tier of states, not the Deep South. That's from Wisconsin east to the Atlantic, then south through the Allegheny and Appalachian mountains to about the South Carolina border," claims Bob Stark, one-time vice-president in charge of lumber purchasing for the

Kansas City-based Frank Paxton Lumber Company, one of the nation's largest marketers of cabinet-grade stock.

And exactly what does "best" mean? Bob Carr, Jr., president of the Educational Lumber Company (EDLCO), a mail-order firm specializing in Appalachian hardwoods, explains. "Hardwood—and softwood, too—from high altitudes or in cold climates—grows slower, is finer in texture, and thus easier to work than the faster-growing, less-dense woods from warmer climates and lower altitudes," he says. "The

Yellow Birch. The largest trees grow in the Canadian provinces of Ontario and Quebec. Smaller trees are harvested in Minnesota and Wisconsin.

Butternut. The best is scattered throughout the northern Great Lakes states and eastern Canada.

Black Cherry. The finest cherry comes out of the Allegheny Mountains in Pennsylvania, and to some extent, West Virginia.

Hard (sugar) maple. The northern tier of Great Lakes states from Wisconsin and Michigan east to New Hampshire (and eastern Canada) produce hard maple commercially.

White Ash. Softer stock hails from Louisiana and Mississippi; harder wood with finer texture from Kentucky, Ohio, and Tennessee.

slower-growing trees also have tighter [more even] grain and are less likely to be discolored from mineral deposits. In fact, the reason we are located in Asheville, North Carolina, is because this [the Appalachians] is where a lot of the good wood grows."

Of course, trees depend on soil nutrients, moisture, and climate for their existence. But within those needs, every species has a unique set of demands to achieve the optimum attributes that woodworkers prefer. That's why, even within a geographical region, some

conditions prove better for the growth of quality hardwood than others. Choice white oak, red oak, and walnut, for instance, tend to anchor in the humus-covered bedrock (preferably limestone) of north-facing slopes, where moisture clings and coolness reigns.

But, even given these species' preferences for growing conditions within their range, those who commercially buy hardwoods and other trees on the stump still migrate toward traditional sources that deliver an abundance (rather than just a few trees) of the good

wood. The map shown *opposite* and *above* illustrates the present origins of the most popular woodworking hardwoods and softwoods, according to the wood experts we talked to.

"That's good to know," you say, "but how can I find out where the wood I want to buy comes from?" It's simple. Just ask. Reliable dealers have your satisfaction in mind. They know where the best wood in a species comes from, and they purchase it there if they possibly can.

PRESSURE-TREATED WOOD

A scary thing happens every time we answer a question about pressure-treated wood in our "Ask *WOOD*®" department: Without fail, each answer sprouts at least three more questions. We've often won-dered out loud if we could ever satisfy all reader questions about this topic.

Knowing that many of you build outdoor projects, we feel it's high time we all became more knowl-edgeable about pressure-treated wood—green wood as some call it. This article focuses only on lumber treated with chromated copper arsenate (CCA)—the most common wood preservative homeowners handle. Later, you'll read more about wood-preserving chemicals.

Since its introduction more than 50 years ago, pressure-treatment has been wood's best friend for defending attacks from termites, other insects, fungal decay, and rot. Not surprisingly, use of treated wood—both indoors and outdoors—has continued to grow to nearly 300 million cubic feet annually. But perhaps because the Environmental Protection Agency (EPA) didn't issue its final determination on treated wood until 1984, myths swirled around the safety of treated wood. Some rumors still exist.

Inside a treating plant

Most of the pressure-treated lumber available to homeowners contains chromated copper arsenate (CCA). Chromium fixes the chemicals in the wood fiber, copper acts as a fungicide, and arsenate is toxic to wood-gobbling termites.

Arsenate sends shivers up some people's backs, but CCA-treated wood contains inorganic pentavalent arsenate or arsenic pentoxide—not the deadly trivalent arsenic used in *Arsenic and Old Lace,* for example. Small amounts of arsenate appear naturally in shrimp, tomatoes, corn, and other foods.

Here's how the chemical solution becomes bonded in the wood: Wood must be dried to 25 percent moisture content or lower before it can be properly treated. At the pressure-treating facility, employees slide a stack of dried dimensional lumber into a steel pressure cylinder (an average cylinder holds up to 30,000 board feet of lumber). After tightly sealing the tank, a vacuum pump sucks air from the cylinder—and the wood cells. Within minutes, the preservative solution floods the cylinder.

Next, a pressure pump forces more solution into the cylinder—and deep into the wood—until the cylinder pressure reaches 140–180 pounds per square inch. The entire process, called a charge, takes from one to two hours.

After pumps draw off excess solution, the cylinder opens and stickered wood begins kiln- or air-drying to about 19 percent. The lumber has a yellow cast when it leaves the cylinder. Within hours, though, the wood color changes to the familiar green shade. As the lumber dries, the preservative components react chemically with each other and bond in the wood cells.

When CCA lumber first appeared in the 1930s, some people occasionally noticed an undesirable greenish-white salt residue. Later, the Koppers Company (now the Hickson Corporation) altered their Wolman formula to eliminate the residue. In addition to appearance benefits, metal hardware and fasteners last longer in CCA oxide-treated wood than with the salt process. Major firms, including Weyerhaeuser and Osmose, followed suit.

How safe is pressure-treated wood?

Earlier this year, we bought a treated 2x4x8' board at five lumberyards and home centers. Through an industry-wide voluntary consumer awareness program, retailers *should* offer EPA-approved "Consumer Information Sheets" to purchasers of treated lumber. These sheets outline safe use of CCA-treated wood. However, two home centers didn't offer the information. Two lumberyards did furnish the sheets, and one home center prominently displayed a sign: "Ask for Information about Treated Lumber."

The biggest treated-wood concern we've noted revolves around leaching questions. After a 10-year study, the EPA ruled CCA-treated wood safe for interior use, play structures, garden edging, and tomato and vineyard stakes. It's safe to eat at CCA-treated picnic tables, but the EPA doesn't recommend CCA-treated wood surfaces for daily food preparations such as countertops or cutting

boards. And, unless you eat wood, it's unlikely exposure to CCA-treated wood will increase one's risk of cancer.

No, CCA-treated wood doesn't emit vapors or odor. However, the ash from burned treated wood could present a health or environmental hazard if not properly handled. For this reason, you should dispose of scraps and sawdust through trash pickup services. The consumer information sheets do warn of inhaling treated-wood sawdust and recommend wearing dust masks and washing hands after handling treated wood—as you should with any nontreated wood.

Let the buyer beware

You do yourself a disservice by specifying only for treated wood at the lumber counter. Ask questions!

What species? Southern pine has become a leader in treated wood because its cell structure seems ideally suited to accept the solution. However, treaters in the West use a lot of ponderosa pine. But, not all lumber treats as well as these two species. Each piece of wood you buy should have a grade stamp that tells the species, grade, and moisture content when inspected.

For deck flooring, some lumberyards recommend only No. 1 lumber. Because the top grade has fewer knots and flaws, it should be less susceptible to warping and twisting. For a 12x12' deck, the additional cost between No. 2 and No. 1 grades should be less than $20. We think it's money well spent for the better grade—and fewer problems.

If you buy CCA-treated wood at an unbelievably low price, don't be surprised by the quality. In fact, you may have a hard time finding a grade stamp on some bargain-priced lumber. According to David Hoak, who owns a CCA-treating facility in Rock Island, Illinois, "If
continued

PRESSURE-TREATED WOOD
continued

you treat garbage wood, you'll have garbage wood that will last a long time."

Also, consider ¾x6 radiused lumber for decking material. In addition to saving money, this treated wood earns high marks on appearance without giving up strength to span typical deck configurations.

What retention level? Look for a second stamp or tag that tells who treated the wood. You'll learn the retention level by reading the treater's stamp. Wood treated for above-ground use will have 0.25 pound per cubic foot of oxides. Wood intended for ground contact will have in excess of 0.40 pound per cubic foot of oxides—roughly 2 ounces in a 2x4x8'.

Apparently because the 0.40 lumber has nearly twice the oxides of 0.25 lumber, some woodworkers incorrectly use the term "double-treated." In practice, after treated lumber dries, it isn't treated again to a higher level. Be sure to look for a stamp or tag that indicates appropriate use on each piece you buy.

Deck-building tips

Before you start nailing down treated wood, review the consumer information sheet and study the installation pamphlets provided by the treater. Many do-it-yourselfers have found out—too late—that they overlooked these important treated-wood guidelines:

Check local building codes. Before you drive the first nail, make sure you build according to your municipal or county regulations.

Fasten bark-side up. Lee Gatzke, *WOOD*® magazine's art director, can point to the boards on his deck that he mistakenly fastened with the bark side down. "They're the warped boards," Lee says. Even if you have to sand off an ugly grade stamp that appears

on the bark side, follow this important guideline whenever possible.

Build with hot-dipped galvanized nails/screws. Moisture and weather demand fasteners that stand up to the elements. Use 12d spiral or ring-shanked nails on nominal decking. Some lumbermen even recommend 2½" deck screws. "I've had twisted CCA wood that pulls out 16-penny galvanized nails," says Terry Fenimore, who builds projects for our sister magazine, *Weekend Woodworking Projects*®. "It's that strong."

Drill holes. Even if you nail together treated wood, take the time to drill pilot holes close to the ends of lumber. That's your best insurance against unsightly splits.

Don't hurry finishes. Treated wood weathers to a gray-green, but some homeowners prefer other colors. Just as with untreated wood, treated wood must be surface dry before a brushed or sprayed finish will adhere. John Cashmore of Weyerhaeuser recommends that "you not paint or stain until the *bottom* of the board is dry to touch. We suggest you wait two to four weeks before finishing."

You can stain or paint treated wood, but if you do, follow manufacturer's instructions. Look for water repellents specifically designed for pressure-treated wood.

In select locations, Hickson Corporation has introduced Wolmanized Extra, a premium-price, pressure-treating solution containing water repellents. Unlike brush-on repellents that treat only the surface, Wolmanized Extra penetrates the entire board. And, expect Osmose to step up promotion of their 15-year-old Weather Shield wood with the same benefits. Neither product permanently protects wood; you'll need to brush on repellents in two to three years. And, Cashmore

cautions that some paint or stain won't adhere well to wood treated with water repellents.

Maintenance. Decks—just like cars—require regular care to battle the effects of sun and moisture. Your investment in outdoor wood deserves an annual or biannual cleaning and recoating with water repellents. Most major franchisers also sell rejuvenating solutions.

Warranty. Major firms back up their products with warranties—up to lifetime limited warranties for as long as you own your home. Before you buy, find out if the chemical company stands behind its product.

Need more information?

For general information about CCA-treated wood:

• **American Wood Preservers Institute.** Free Consumer Information Sheets and *Questions and Answers About Treated Wood.* 1945 Old Gallows Road, Suite 550, Vienna, VA 22182.

• **Osmose.** For deck-building pamphlets and CCA information, call 800-522-WOOD.

• **Weyerhaeuser.** *All You Need to Know About Wood That Goes Outdoors,* call 800-548-5767.

• **Wolmanized Wood.** *How to Build a Deck* and *Straight Talk on the Safety and Use of Wolmanized Wood,* $2 ppd. from Hickson Corporation, 426 Seventh Ave., Room 750, Pittsburgh, PA 15219.

• **Regulatory Information.** Environmental Protection Agency, Office of Pesticide Programs, Mail Stop H7508C, 401 M St. SW, Washington, DC 20460.

WHAT YOU SHOULD KNOW ABOUT TOXIC WOOD

During the Middle Ages, English archers frequently developed a rash from their yew longbows. Some musicians of the 1930s broke out after playing woodwind instruments—called recorders—crafted of cocobolo. But, don't panic. According to a *WOOD*® magazine reader and poison expert, your chance of a toxic reaction to one or more domestic wood species is as infrequent as 1 in 100. And, to reduce those odds even more, he points to guilty wood, tells you what to expect, and advises you how to avoid problems.

Editor's note: Frankly, I was never too concerned regarding toxic wood. Heck, I've made it through four decades without even catching poison ivy! But, about two weeks before I sat down to write this footnote, my arms carried an ugly rash. As far as my physician and I could determine, it came from cocobolo. One day I was preparing some cocobolo boards for "Wood Profile" photos. Later, the rash showed up. Nothing else in my routine had been out of the ordinary—except for the cocobolo. I guess I'm extremely sensitive. The rash gradually disappeared, along with any longing I might have had to one day work that beautiful wood.
—Peter J. Stephano
Features Editor

Toxic wood through the ages

For centuries, it's been fairly common knowledge that some woods, and things made from them, could hinder your health. As far back as 60 A.D., for instance, the Roman historian and naturalist Pliny the Elder described a case where four soldiers actually died after drinking wine from hip flasks made of yew.

Of lesser gravity was the experience of a few German sawyers in the early 1700s. It seems they developed chronic irritation of the nose and eyes, as well as headaches, from sawing bald cypress.

Historic reports such as these—combined with current medical knowledge concerning allergies and irritants—add up to incriminating evidence for several species.

What are your chances of a reaction to wood? Statistics say that only two to five percent of all people develop an allergic sensitivity to one or more compounds found in wood. But, if you handle a lot of potentially toxic species, and work with them long enough, you increase your chances of an allergic reaction. And, with sufficient exposure (that varies individually), some woods bother everyone.

What kind of a reaction can you expect? Your body will respond to toxic wood in one or more of the following ways:
- skin and eye irritations;
- respiratory problems;
- nausea, headache, general ill-feeling, liver or kidney malfunction;
- cancer of the nose and sinuses (*nasopharyngeal carcinoma*).

Sometimes wood just stuffs you up

Any dust, including wood dust, mildly irritates the sensitive mucous membranes of your nose and eyes, making you sneeze and tear. The dust of some woods, such as western red cedar and rosewood, can be especially bothersome. Jim Boelling, *WOOD*® magazine's project builder, recalls an uncomfortable instance of working rosewood: "The shop was hot, and the rosewood immediately made my nose stuffy and my eyes water—like being exposed to tear gas in Navy boot camp."

However, other woods can make you even more uncomfortable, with a rash that doctors classify as either *irritant dermatitis* or *allergic dermatitis*. Woods called *primary irritants* cause the first type. And, primary irritants provoke reactions in anyone, if you handle them long enough. The rash usually has a uniformly red, swollen area that may erupt in blisters. Typically, it first shows up on the webs of skin between your fingers, where perspiration deposited the toxin from the wood dust and it contacts the skin. Satinwood and snakewood are two woods proven to be primary irritants (for others, see the chart on *page 23*).

For you to get an allergic-type rash, you first must be allergy-prone to one or more of the chemicals found in certain woods called sensitizers. And, it may take repeated contact for your body to develop a great enough allergy for it to react—the so-called "latency period" of as little as 5 days and up to 6–8 months. Because individuals have different immune systems and content of the sensitizing compound varies in each piece of wood, it's hard to say how much contact will spur a reaction. But, if you eventually do react, the rash will look like poison ivy—red with small, individual, itchy bumps. The rosewoods, particularly, can produce allergic reactions.

continued

WHAT YOU SHOULD KNOW ABOUT TOXIC WOOD
continued

Stock that takes your breath away

Following an earthquake in 1923, the Japanese rebuilt the small village of Beisugi with western red cedar. Not long after, nearly 40 percent of the villagers developed severe respiratory symptoms while in their homes—symptoms that cleared up when villagers went outdoors. Allergists now call the affliction "Beisugi asthma."

As with species that irritate the skin, wood that can cause respiratory problems falls into the two categories of primary irritants and sensitizers. With respiratory problems, though, primary irritants pose less of a threat. That's mainly due to your body's efficiency in preventing wood dust from entering the lungs in significant quantities, or eliminating it by coughing once it does enter. In fact, medical research has yet to pinpoint any species as a primary irritant causing respiratory reactions.

Although you may escape primary irritants, you have a far better chance of developing an allergic reaction to one or more of the many woods that act as respiratory sensitizers. These include western red cedar of Beisugi fame, redwood, rosewood, mahogany, ebony, myrtle, birch, and others.

If even a small amount of dust from one of these sensitizers enters the lungs of an allergic individual, the air passage becomes irritated and swells, a condition frequently indistinguishable from asthma. The symptoms also can include anything from a mild cough and heaviness in the chest that resembles a minor cold, to severe wheezing and the inability to breathe. Symptoms of this condition go away when you're not exposed to the wood, but return when you come back to the shop to work.

Molds frequently trigger reactions, too. One that actually grows *in* wood happens to be extremely potent: *cryptostroma corticale*. This mold lives happily between the bark and sapwood of many hardwood trees, especially favoring maple and birch. It's responsible for the marbleized spalting that woodturners prize, and for "maple bark stripper's disease," a condition with all the symptoms of severe respiratory allergy. Among hobby woodworkers, at least one death has been reported, that of a New Orleans man in 1987.

There are two more molds that sometimes cause serious allergic reactions. *Aspergillus nigricant* and *alternaria*, though, prefer moist, dark places, such as a sawdust pile in a basement corner.

Pass the pepto, please, the species didn't agree

Many woods, among them birch, black locust, and padauk, contain compounds that, when ingested in sufficient quantities (including inhalation), prove capable of producing any one of several systemic reactions: nausea, vomiting, headache, kidney failure, hallucinations, or cardiac problems. As a matter of fact, native Americans brewed the bark and sapwood of mimosa, a small tree in the black locust family, for a tea that induced relaxation and sleep.

Do you have an aspirin allergy? Then, be wary of willow and birch. Very sensitive individuals might only need casual exposure, such as a whiff of sawdust, to react, since both species possess significant concentrations of *salicylic acid*, the predecessor of aspirin. And from history, we know that two species, yew and oleander, contain enough of the toxins called *cardiac glycosides*, similar to the heart drug digitalis, to be extremely dangerous even in tiny amounts. Luckily for woodworkers, the greatest concentration of the toxins is in the leaves, berries, and bark.

That leads us to wood dust, and cancer. Among woodworkers, the chances of developing nasal and sinus cancer run about five to 10,000—40 times greater than nonwoodworkers.

Never say no to a dust mask

Although researchers haven't identified the cancer-causing compound—primarily because the disease has a latency period of from 30 to 50 years—some evidence points to dust from wood with high tannin content. Such species include chestnut, oak, redwood, western red cedar, and hemlock.

If you have worked wood for more than 25 years, *any* recurrent nasal discharge, bleeding, or sinus infection could signal this condition. Report it to a physician.

Tips to tackle toxicity

Despite the evidence, most woodworkers have never experienced serious reactions to wood. So, don't let possible toxicity scare you. Instead, know the properties of the woods you want to work. Refer to the chart, *right*, to find potential troublemakers.

"If you take to the woods to harvest your stock," says poison expert Robert Woodcock, "keep the following points in mind to avoid or limit your exposure."

continued

WOOD WITH A RECORD

WOOD SPECIES	TOXIC CLASS		REACTION				POTENCY			SOURCE			INCIDENCE		
	Irritant	Sensitizer	Respiratory	Eye & Skin	Nausea, Etc.	Nasal Cancer	Little	Great	Extreme	Leaves, Bark	Dust	Wood	Unknown	Rare	Common
Bald cypress		X	X				X				X			X	
Balsam fir		X		X			X				X			X	
Beech		X		X				X		X				X	
Birch		X	X		X			X			X	X		X	
Black locust	X				X			X		X				X	
Blackwood		X		X				X			X	X			X
Boxwood		X	X				X				X	X		X	
Cashew		X		X				X			X	X		X	
Cocobolo	X		X	X				X			X	X			X
Dahoma		X	X					X			X				X
Ebony	X		X	X				X			X	X			X
Elm		X		X			X				X			X	
Goncalo alves		X		X			X				X	X		X	
Greenheart		X	X	X					X		X	X			X
Hemlock						X		X		X	X			X	
Iroko	X		X	X					X		X	X			X
Mahogany		X	X	X			X				X			X	
Mansonia	X		X	X					X		X	X			X
Maple		X	X					X			X	X		X	
Mimosa	X				X				X	X	X	X			X
Myrtle		X	X					X		X	X	X			X
Oak, red						X		X			X			X	
Obeche		X	X	X				X			X				X
Oleander	X				X				X	X	X	X		X	
Olivewood		X	X	X				X			X	X			X
Opepe		X	X				X				X			X	
Padauk	X		X	X	X				X		X	X			X
Pau ferro		X		X			X				X	X		X	
Peroba rosa		X	X					X			X	X			X
Purpleheart		X		X	X		X				X	X		X	
Quebracho						X		X			X			X	
Redwood		X	X		X		X				X			X	
Rosewood(s)		X	X	X					X		X	X			X
Satinwood	X		X	X					X		X	X			X
Sassafras		X	X		X	X	X			X	X	X		X	
Sequoia	X		X				X				X	X		X	
Snakewood	X		X					X			X	X		X	
Spruce		X	X				X				X	X		X	
Walnut		X		X			X				X			X	
Wenge		X	X	X				X			X	X			X
Willow		X			X			X		X	X		X		
W. Red Cedar		X	X			X		X			X	X			X
Teak		X		X				X			X				X
Yew, European	X			X				X			X	X			X
Zebrawood		X		X				X			X	X		X	

WHAT YOU SHOULD KNOW ABOUT TOXIC WOOD
continued

• **Harvest only in fall or winter.** Trees cut when the sap is up have higher toxicity.

• **Claim the heartwood.** With most toxic species, the leaves and stems contain the most toxin, followed by the bark, the sapwood, then the heartwood.

• **Season toxic wood.** Wood worked green causes more skin reactions because the sawdust clings.

Woodcock also insists on adequate shop ventilation. "It keeps the work space cool and your perspiration down, decreasing the dust's contact time with your skin." In addition, a well-ventilated shop discourages the growth of mold spores. And, consider installing a dust collection system. Even then, you should always wear a tight-fitting, government-approved (NIOSH) dust mask if you plan to raise large amounts of wood dust.

"Don't neglect cleanliness," Woodcock continues. "It's a good idea to frequently wash, or even shower, when working a possibly toxic wood. Creases and skin pores, as well as dirty hair, trap fine dust particles, inviting reaction. For extra protection, apply a barrier cream, such as DuPont's Protek."

Finally, he urges, "Whenever you develop a *persistent* set of symptoms, especially when you can connect them with exposure to a wood [remember, symptoms may be delayed 12 hours], contact a physician, allergist, dermatologist, or specialist in industrial medicine. And, be sure to mention that you're a woodworker.

"Of course, potentially toxic woods should never be used for functional bowls, goblets, trays, or any other object likely to hold food," notes the specialist. Even using the wood for jewelry has caused problems.

For answers to problems regarding toxic wood reactions, call one of the regional poison control centers (PCC) *below.*

New York City PCC
212-340-4494

Delaware Valley PCC
Philadelphia, Pennsylvania
215-386-2100

Georgia PCC
Atlanta, Georgia
404-589-4400

Regional Poison Control System
Cincinnati, Ohio
513-558-5111

Mid-Plains Poison Center
Omaha, Nebraska
402-390-5400

Texas State Poison Center
Galveston, Texas
409-765-9728

Arizona Poison Control System
Tucson, Arizona
602-626-6016

Rocky Mountain Poison & Drug Center
Denver, Colorado
303-629-1123

UCDMC Davis Regional PCC
Sacramento, California
916-453-3692

Oregon Poison Center
Portland, Oregon
503-279-8968

FOREST WOOD FREE FOR THE HAULING

It's unique, unexpected, and—to top it all off—free (or nearly so). Found wood is everywhere, and as we discovered, you can work it into some dazzling projects. Here's a report by features editor Peter J. Stephano, the ham in the photos *above.*

You'll never buy wood like it at the lumberyard or hardwood retailer because what we call "found wood" never leaves the forest, at least commercially. Loggers and lots of other folks consider burls, crotches, partially decayed or bug-riddled wood, and practically all downed trees as waste wood, or, at best, firewood.

Don't let this wood's humble status deceive you, however. Beneath an often drab, dirt-covered exterior you may discover sound, attractively grained (sometimes even spectacular) wood that is dry and workable. Of course, there's always the possibility that much of what you come across will be too decayed, too smashed and broken, or too waterlogged to fool with.

What you'll find

Besides free specimens of all the commercially harvested hardwoods (walnut, maple, oak, etc.) that grow where you live, you'll happen upon wood not usually offered for sale. These real forest gems include:

• **Spalted wood.** Beginning wood decay in many species tints grain with the colorful swirls and patterns of marble (maple, beech, birch, and box elder spalt with phenomenal beauty).

• **Burls.** Sometimes called burrs, burls appear as rounded, woody outgrowths on tree trunks. Inside, these swirls from ill-fated buds provide an astounding grain figure.

• **Crotches.** The area just below the separation of the trunk into twins shows intriguing figure when sliced lengthwise.

• **Root stock.** The ball at the tree base that starts about 1' above the ground and extends 1' below ground level contains heartwood and sapwood intertwined for a special grain effect.

• **Bug wood.** Tunneled, bored-out, wooden residences of powder-post beetles and grubs, if structurally sound, can make eye-pleasing projects.

For decades, vacationers have collected driftwood, perhaps the classic found wood, in its sand-washed, sun-bleached variations of form and texture. West Coast wood seekers, particularly Californians, harvest the iron-hard, richly hued root burl of the manzanita shrub, then turn it for outstanding vases and bowls (see *page 27*).

Scouting found wood

In urban areas, found and free wood may be as close as your doorstep or a neighbor's yard in the guise of a dead shade-tree limb. A call to your city forester's office also can turn up piles of downed, dry stock that once may have graced boulevards. Also try these sources: tree service companies, construction sites, power companies (they trim trees for line maintenance), and county landfills.

Rural areas provide a bountiful harvest in wooded public and private lands (get permission first). Slashings left from logging operations provide tree parts too disfigured, gnarled, or short to haul out (check with sawmills listed in the Yellow Pages to find loggers' names or ask around at a chain saw dealer). Other sources include commercial fruit orchards, local sawmills for discards, highway maintenance departments, farm woodlots and hedgerows, river-fed lakes, wooded stream banks, and beaches.

Spotting the good stuff

You want dry wood, but how can you tell if it's dry enough? Clearly, a pocket moisture meter

continued

FOREST WOOD FREE FOR THE HAULING
continued

Photo *above:* You may not always be able to make a silk purse from a sow's ear, but you certainly can turn waste wood into some super pieces. All of these projects came from free, found wood: (1) fishing rod rack from a scrap of old rough-sawn elm board with crotch figure; (2) butternut bowl from firewood scrap; (3) spalted maple weed pot; (4) bowl of decayed walnut crotch; (5) buggy butternut pencil holder; (6) one-drawer jewelry box from walnut burl; (7) band-sawn and bored-out spalted maple change boxes; (8) rolling pin from maple firewood; (9) spalted maple belt buckle; (10) compartmented earring box of spalted beech; (11) fire-scorched and spalted hickory pencil/note holder; (12) walnut bud vase; (13) osage orange vase.

is your best bet. If you don't own one (they cost about $100), you'll have to make an educated guess based on weight. Dry wood will be a lot lighter than green. Even better, bring along a belt hatchet and rap the wood with the flat end (if a sawed end is exposed, hit it there). A resonant "knock" is a

fairly good indicator of dryness—green wood sounds rather dull.

Rapping with a hatchet can also tell you if a burl or a limb contains a worthless, decayed core. To be sure, cut into it with your saw for a peek into the wood that will confirm or deny its soundness. If the wood is spalted, you'll see the dark-lined pattern.

Often, good wood may be decomposing on the outside (in the sapwood), and yet have a solid, workable heartwood. In cases like this, inspect the cut ends of the piece to check for a solid core. Then cut off the sapwood to salvage heartwood.

Sometimes downed wood, and especially driftwood, will be wet from ground moisture or even completely waterlogged. If it looks, feels, and sounds otherwise solid, bring it home despite the moisture; it will remain just as solid after proper drying.

Note: We suggest you focus on found wood that is already dry. Dry wood requires less care and preparation before working than green wood. Finding, cutting, seasoning (drying), and storing green wood to make it stable requires special knowledge and techniques, some of which are discussed on pages 28 and 42. For now, bring home wood that fits in one of the Three D's—down, dead, or dying. Also, unless you're equipped for logging, seek only short bolts (sections of a tree limb or trunk) and pieces you can cut free with a bow, pruning, or small chain saw and can carry yourself.

Preserving your found wood

Follow these simple steps to preserve and finish seasoning your "finds":

1. Before you take wood home, remove the bark. This leaves pests where you found them and makes for cleaner, neater stacking later. Also chop away any decayed, soft (punky) wood and leave it behind.

2. Apply a sealer to any freshly sawn ends. End grain both absorbs moisture and frees it faster than wood around the bolt. This results in cracking and the tiny fissures called checks that develop during the stress of rapid drying. The U.S. Forest Products Laboratory recommends aluminum paint in a spar varnish base or asphalt roofing cement as an end coating.

Two woodworkers we know, Dale Nish of Provo, Utah, and Jim Woodruff of Denver, Colorado, use a commercial wood sealer, Mobilicer-M, but advise that either paraffin or paste wax works, too. An Iowa wood collector, Allen Pratt, says shellac works for him.

Other sealers vary from thinned white glue to oil-base paint. Whatever you use, coating the ends (and about 1" up onto the sides) allows the wood to continue drying gradually.

Note: Split larger chunks, or rounds, of wood in half lengthwise to expose the pith (dark center core of immature wood). Then chop out the pith to prevent decay and coat the end grain.

3. Treat riddled wood for insects. Buggy wood still may be actively infested, and the critters can spread to other wood. If you want to save your find, heat it in an oven or microwave (slowly) to 130° F. to kill the pests, or use a spray pesticide.

Storing your stash

For the first month or two (how long depends on whether or not your dry wood is damp), it's wise to stack your found wood outside, cordwood fashion, so the air can circulate through it. If you've ever stacked firewood, you know what we mean, off the ground, with enough space to let the wind blow through, and the top of the pile covered with a plastic tarp.

After this initial stacking, or seasoning, period, bring the wood indoors until you want to use it. But keep it off damp basement floors and out of places with high humidity. Ideally, to avoid checks, your storage spot should closely approximate the atmospheric conditions where the wood will be worked and finally displayed.

Many woodworkers have great results with air-dried wood. Others insist that wood must be kiln-dried to adequately reduce its moisture and make it stable. Without your own kiln, you'll have to store your wood where it will remain dry and you can monitor it for good results.

Possibilities for found wood

What can you make with found wood? The items photographed for this article should give you some ideas, but your newly discovered stock really has few limitations— size may be one, the amount of degrade (checking and cracking during seasoning) the other.

Use your found wood as individual project pieces, or as stock to be resawn as parts of many pro-

jects (the latter especially if you initially split larger chunks into squares for drying). With a fence on a bandsaw or a special jig on a tablesaw you can reduce spalted wood, burls, and crotch wood into thinner stock ideal for exquisite jewelry box tops, belt buckles, or inlay work. Look to the wood, and let it suggest alternatives.

The Magnificent Manzanita

Sculptured marble? Ceramics? Neither—but this turned vase of manzanita root burl has characteristics of both. Found primarily in Mexico and California at elevations above 1,000 feet, manzanita is a hardwood shrub with a dense, gnarled root system. At the base of the root is the burl (shown in inset). With tendrils and thin roots trimmed off, the burl can be worked into fascinating and colorful turnings, bases, and even tabletops (some burls reach 3' in diameter).

However, working manzanita isn't easy. The roots often grow around rocks that remain undetected until hit by a woodworking tool.

In California, a Forest Service permit (free) allows you to dig a few pieces in designated areas. Manzanita also is available by mail order from Shir-Lee Manzanita Ranch, Inc., Dept. W, P.O. Box 6, Potrero, CA 92063.

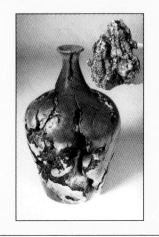

HOW TO TRANSFORM FOUND WOOD INTO USABLE STOCK

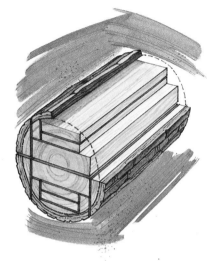

Now you can add substantially to your lumber stockpile for future projects—at little or no cost. And we think you'll have lots of fun doing it, too!

WOOD®—On the road again

Although we've published articles about freshly cut wood over the years in *WOOD*® magazine, one question still remained in my mind. "How do you section and cut your way from an irregular-shaped hunk of wood to stock you can actually use to make something with?"

Not long ago, I seized my opportunity to find out. It happened when Marlen Kemmet, *WOOD*® magazine's how-to editor, passed along a hot tip from two of our readers. They had spotted "some of the best quilted maple they had ever seen" less than 120 miles from Des Moines. Marlen and Jim Downing, our design editor, wanted to take a look-see, so we loaded up our gear one Saturday morning and headed down Interstate 80 to Iowa City.

It was there, all right—more freshly cut maple than we could hope to carry! After debarking the logs and sealing their cut surfaces

and end grain to prevent rapid moisture loss and further splitting, we muscled as many of them as we could into the back of Jim's pickup. (That's Jim and me hefting the logs into the truck in the photo *above*. Marlen, at rest on the tailgate of Jim's truck, apparently was on his break when this photo was taken.) A few hours later, back in Des Moines, we tossed off our bounty outside the *WOOD*® magazine offices. And the following Monday, we started our investigation of what turned out to be a most intriguing process.

Well, that's how our adventure began. But there's lots more to the

story, so be sure to read on to find out how we transformed those big chunks of maple into workable pieces. Here's hoping you find the process as interesting as we did.
—*Larry Clayton*
Editor

Start by sectioning the logs

Since the slabs of wood we had lugged back to our offices were much too large to handle, our first task was to section them. And it didn't take us long to find out that you can't just divide up a log any old way you want. No, sir!

That's where knowing how to "read a log" comes in mighty handy. And fortunately for us, Jim Boelling, our project builder, has done quite a lot of log-splitting and was able to pass along some helpful tips. "Basically, you need to attack wood from its most vulnerable points—along the cracks that invariably occur during the drying process," Jim advised. "Think of it as exploiting the wood's weakness." Typically, the larger the log you're working with, the more stress cracks you will see.

Start by lifting the piece you plan to work on up to a comfortable height. (We sat ours on another slab.) Now, looking down onto the top of the log, determine which cracks you want to attack. Major fissures often will show down the side of the log as well as from the end.

Once you've settled on your course of action, begin driving a pair of wedges down into the top of the log as shown in the photo *above.* As you drive in the wedges, the sections of the log should separate; often, they pop apart under impact. Divide the log into as many sections as there are major cracks.

Here's an important safety reminder:

Be sure to exercise all reasonable caution when sectioning your logs. Note that Jim Downing has donned a face shield to deflect flying wood chips, as well as gloves to protect his hands from a glancing blow of the sledge.

Make yourself a shooting box

With any luck at all, you now have several workable sections that need further processing. But wait a minute! Since none of the surfaces is flat enough to allow machining, you need to build what we call a "shooting box." This simple-to-construct jig makes it possible for you to shave one of the log's surfaces flat with the help of a router. The Exploded View drawing *above* shows how the various jig parts fit together.

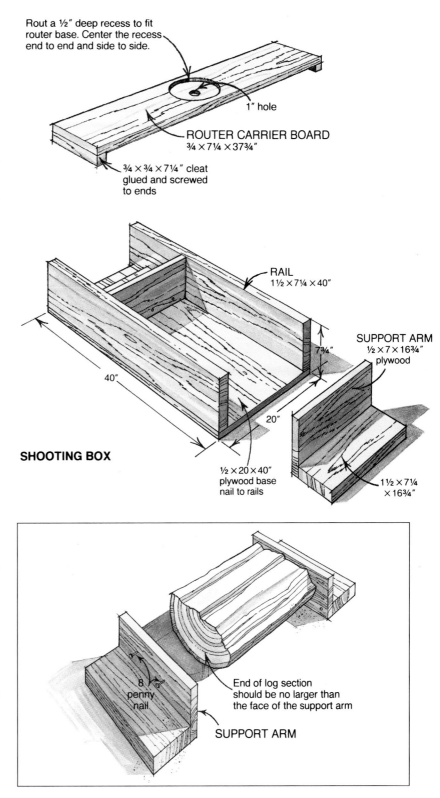

Rout a ½" deep recess to fit router base. Center the recess end to end and side to side.

1" hole

ROUTER CARRIER BOARD
¾ × 7¼ × 37¾"

¾ × ¾ × 7¼" cleat glued and screwed to ends

RAIL
1½ × 7¼ × 40"

SUPPORT ARM
½ × 7 × 16¾"
plywood

40"

7¾"

20"

SHOOTING BOX

½ × 20 × 40" plywood base nail to rails

1½ × 7¼ × 16¾"

8 penny nail

End of log section should be no larger than the face of the support arm

SUPPORT ARM

continued

HOW TO TRANSFORM FOUND WOOD INTO USABLE STOCK
continued

Processing your wood—the five key steps

Once you've completed construction of the shooting box, you're now ready for the exciting part—remolding those awkward-shaped pieces of wood into project material. Ready to start?

1. Begin by nailing one of the shooting box's support arms to the log as shown in the sketch on the *previous page*. Make sure that the top edge of the arm extends slightly above the surface of the log. Repeat this process to attach the second arm to the log.

Now, lift the log into position in the shooting box. Also, locate the router-mounted carrier board atop the rails of the shooting box. Lower the router's cutter (we used a ½" carbide-tipped straight bit) so that it will remove about ¼" of material. Then, holding the router as shown in Photo 1, move the carrier board back and forth over the log until you have removed the stock.

2. Actually, from here on out, you can rely on your bandsaw, fitted with the widest blade you have, to make the remaining cuts. As you can see by looking at Photo 2, you make the next cut with the surface that you just trued-up against the bandsaw table. Use a straight-edged guide board to control your cut. Take your time here; the slower you go, the straighter your cut will be.

Note: *Due to the thickness of our log section, we had to remove a portion of it with a chainsaw prior to making the cut shown. Only then would the remaining piece pass under the upper blade guide. You should usually remove the core of heartwood from log pieces.*

3. Next, with two (in our case, three) flat surfaces to work with, you can call on the saw's rip fence to guide your remaining cuts. To determine the maximum-width cut you can make on your machine,

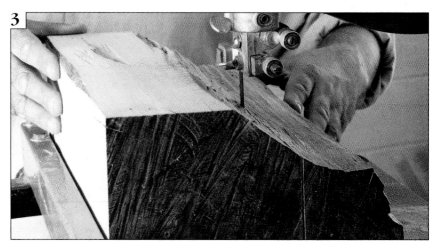

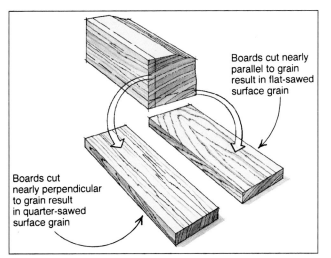

Boards cut nearly parallel to grain result in flat-sawed surface grain

Boards cut nearly perpendicular to grain result in quarter-sawed surface grain

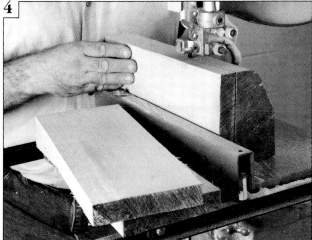

raise the upper blade guide up as far as possible and measure the distance from the table to the bottom of the blade guide. Then, set your rip fence that distance from the blade, and pass the stock through the saw again as shown in Photo 3.

4. At this point, you have some decision-making to do. If you want to make turning squares or bowl blanks with the wood, simply surface the fourth edge by running it through the saw again. Then, cut the material to the desired configurations. If we had chosen to, we could have ripped the chunk shown in Photo 3 into several turning squares. Or, we could have crosscut it into a few bowl blanks. If you want to produce some flat stock, however, we recommend that you spend some time deciding which edge of the material to cut your boards from. Why? Because how you do it will affect the appearance of your boards. As you can see by looking at the drawing *above*, if you quarter-saw the stock, you'll end up with boards that display a straight grain pattern. But if you prefer the cathedral grain pattern of flat-sawed boards, that's fine, too.

What's a good way to determine how to proceed? We've found that wetting the surfaces of the wood with a damp rag allows us to quickly see which grain pattern looks most pleasing.

Once you've made your decision, set your bandsaw's fence the desired distance from the blade. (Shrinking and additional machining will reduce each board dimension by about ⅛" or so. Be sure to allow for this reduction.) Rip the material into boards as shown in Photo 4.

5. OK, you've finished sawing your logs into some great-looking boards of various thicknesses, and maybe even some bowl blanks and turning squares. Now what? In order to ensure that you will have usable material when it dries, you need to seal, sticker, and store the wood.

To prevent uneven drying of the material, seal all end grain as shown in Photo 5 with paint or one of the products designed especially for this purpose. (See the Buying Guide for the product we used.) Then, cut several thin, narrow pieces of spacer material—preferably from leftover log scraps. These so-called "stickers," when placed between each layer of stock and near the ends of the boards, allow air to move freely in and around the boards as they dry.

After stickering your freshly cut and prepared lumber, move it to a dry, moderately warm location for storing. Also, label the stacks as to species and stickering date.

How long will it be before your lumber air-dries enough to use it? That depends, but an old adage

calls for one year of drying time per inch of thickness. Of course, this will vary with the drying conditions. By far the best way to judge readiness at any given time is with a moisture meter.

Buying Guide
• **Sealtite.** Green wood sealer, Catalog No. 01W61. For current prices, contact Woodcraft, Dept. WBH, P.O. Box 1686, Parkersburg, WV 26102-1686.

SHOULD YOU BE USING HARDWOOD PLYWOOD?

Perhaps confusion about the quality, grading, and types of hardwood plywood has kept you from using it. If that's the case, you're unnecessarily limiting the scope of your woodworking projects. Here's advice about the pros and cons of working with this unique material.

As early as 3000 B.C., Egyptians bonded thin layers of fine exotic hardwoods to commonplace cores, then worked this ancient version of hardwood plywood into furniture. Their primary purpose in using it was to conserve the hard-to-get exotic woods the pharaoh and other wealthy customers demanded in their furnishings.

Today's material, while it still conserves fine hardwoods, has other attributes that make it ideal for cabinet doors, sides, and tops; bookshelves; drawer bottoms; and other relatively large surfaces.

As with all plywoods, layers are bonded at right angles to each other (crossbanding) for strength and stability. Face and back veneers are about 1/50" thick.

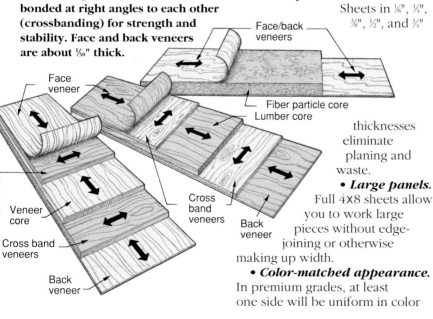

Face veneer
Veneer core
Cross band veneers
Back veneer
Cross band veneers
Back veneer
Face/back veneers
Fiber particle core
Lumber core

Why use hardwood plywood?

Hardwood plywood usually costs more than the equal quantity of solid hardwood, but it can be worth the premium. Among the advantages are:

• *Dimensional stability.* Crossbanded layers (see illustration, *below*) and balanced construction mean that hardwood plywood won't shrink, swell, or warp as much as lumber. Its thin plies, lying at right angles to each other, as well as the various core materials available (see table *opposite*), produce uniform strength both with and across the grain.

Baltic birch, a widely distributed product from the Soviet Union and Scandinavia, has even better strength. All of the plies in this veneer-core product (and there are as many as two more per thickness than other plywoods) are rotary-cut birch and without gaps or voids. In 60" square panels, Baltic birch comes in metric thicknesses approximating 1/4", 3/8", 1/2", 5/8", and 3/4".

• *Variety in thicknesses.* Sheets in 1/8", 1/4", 3/8", 1/2", and 3/4" thicknesses eliminate planing and waste.

• *Large panels.* Full 4x8 sheets allow you to work large pieces without edge-joining or otherwise making up width.

• *Color-matched appearance.* In premium grades, at least one side will be uniform in color

and grain, making staining and finishing easier.

There are some drawbacks

Hardwood plywood does have its limitations. Keep these factors in mind so you can make the best choice:

• *Cost.* Compared to solid stock on a board-foot basis, hardwood plywood definitely is more expensive.

To compute the approximate board foot cost of any panel, first figure the number of board feet it equals. Use the formula *thickness ✕ width ✕ length* (all in inches) *divided by 144.* If you worked the formula on a piece of 3/4"✕48"✕96" flat-sliced red oak plywood, you'd find it equals 24 board feet. If the panel cost $67, you'd divide $67 by 24 for a board foot cost of $2.79. Now compare that to the board-foot price of the best quality First and Second 1" plain-sawn solid red oak, which, let's say, is $2.31 (1" in hardwood grading is the closest you'll come to 3/4"-thick stock).

In the above example, you'd pay 48 cents more per board foot for hardwood plywood. With its performance and working advantages, plywood at this price makes a good choice. But what if the price difference was $1 or more?

• *Limited selection.* Since dealers stock what's in demand, your supplier may only have three or four types of hardwood plywood, such as the popular oaks, birch, and mahogany. You may be able to special-order other types of hardwood veneers, but you'll still be limited to a dozen or so of the most common, and no exotic woods. You might approach your project by first determining the type of hardwood plywood available, *then* selecting the compatible solid stock. This advice also applies to

Types of face veneers

Book matched

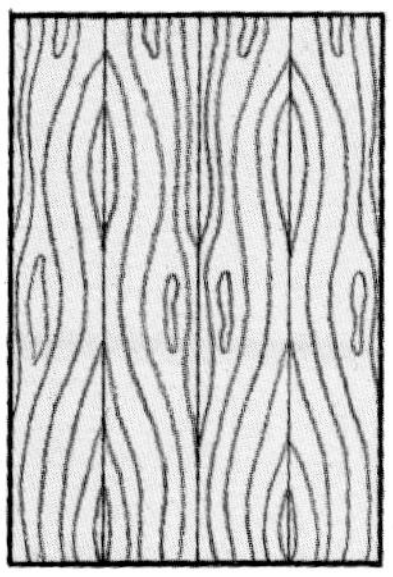

Slip matched

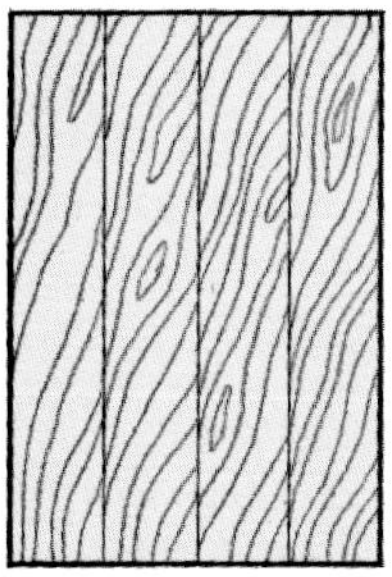

Rotary cut

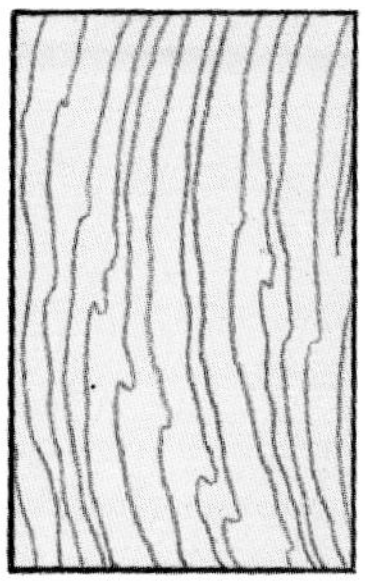

the thin, solid wood edging strips applied where the panel's edge otherwise would show. It's not often carried in more than a half dozen hardwood species.

• ***Unreliable stated thickness.*** The tendency for hardwood plywood panels to vary in thickness from their stated dimension can be frustrating. If you buy a 3/4"-thick panel, for instance, it may stray 1/64" to 1/32" from that thickness. This often is due to the foreign origin of much of this material and the resulting metric thickness measurement, particularly in ash and birch plywood (50 percent or more comes from Taiwan, Japan, and Indonesia). But even among U.S. manufacturers, thickness may vary slightly from batch to batch and mill to mill. You can adjust your measurements, jigs, and cuts to compensate for the variance, but be sure to buy all hardwood plywood for the same project at one time to save resetting.

• ***Thin face veneers.*** U.S.-made hardwood plywood has face veneers averaging 1/30" in thickness. Some species, such as black walnut, are sliced thinner, to 1/32". Foreign veneers are thinner still and can be tough to saw without splintering and sand without destroying.

What are the veneer choices?

Veneers, which are nothing more than scant slices off a log, vary in appearance because of the methods by which they're removed. Oak, birch, ash, and other plentiful species lend themselves to peeling by a large lathe, a process very similar to spinning paper towels from a roll. As with softwood plywood, these *rotary-cut,* continuous slices usually cover a sheet in one piece, producing an erratic grain pattern. Because of this simplified slicing procedure and the elimination of matching and other hand work, rotary-cut veneers cost less.

Flat-sliced veneers come off the log one flitch, or cut, at a time—just as a potato passes through a vegetable slicer. A surface covered with flat-sliced veneer—and almost all common hardwoods are available this way—resembles a series of glued-up boards. This type of veneer is moderately expensive.

Once veneers (other than rotary-cut) have been removed from the log, they must be added to the plywood core. *Match* refers to their arrangement on the face and back. *Slip-matched,* the most common way of applying pieces, has consecutive flitches as they come

continued

HARDWOOD PLYWOOD CORES

Core type	Plies per thickness	How it fastens	How it machines	Comments
Lumber	(5/8" to 3/4") 5 plies	Similar to solid wood. Holds screws and nails well. Requires pilot holes.	Same as solid stock for sawing, edge-forming. Edges can be left exposed.	Expensive, but works most like solid wood. Core pieces run in longest dimension. Can warp across width. Often has hardwood core.
Veneer	(1/8" to 3/4") 3 to 7 plies	Screws and nails hold solidly in front and back. Edges have little holding power and require pilot holes.	Saws well, but core may splinter. Impossible to shape without edge-banding. Requires edge tape.	Provides most strength. Good for all-around use. Fir plies often have voids. Large expanses can warp slightly.
Particle	(3/4") 3 plies	Use finely threaded screws and thin nails. Edges split easily.	Very hard. Requires carbide tools. saws well but veneer can splinter. Edges can be shaped. Core difficult to stain and finish.	Least expensive, but most stable. Heavy. Long shelves or doors will sag without support. Corners may break. Wear dust mask when working.
Fiber	(3/4") 3 plies	Use fine-threaded screws, thin nails. Edges split easily.	Very hard. Needs carbide tools. Edges can be shaped. Saws relatively well. Veneer can splinter. Core hard to stain and finish, requires tape.	Heavy. Weight can sag long pieces. Corners break easily. Fine dust requires use of mask. Core uniformly fine. Stable.

SHOULD YOU BE USING HARDWOOD PLYWOOD?
continued

HARDWOOD PLYWOOD GRADES		
Grade	**Veneer quality**	**Defects allowed**
A—Premium	If sliced, pieces are slip- or book-matched for pleasing effect of color and grain. Can also be one-piece rotary-cut	Minor, but not frequent burls, pin knots, and inconspicuous small patches
1—Good[1]	Unmatched slices permitted, but no sharp contrasts in color, grain, or figure	Burls, slight color streaks, pin knots, and inconspicuous small patches in limited amounts
2—Sound	No figure, color, or grain match	Smooth patches, sound knots, and discoloration or varying color
3—Utility	Reject material	Open knots, splits, wormholes up to 1 inch; major discoloration
4—Backing	Rarely found due to unlimited defects; strength is the only gradable feature	
G1S[2]	Dealer-applied designation meaning "Good 1 Side" used primarily for foreign-origin plywood of ¼" or less thickness; face can be good to premium, back with large defects or of another hardwood species	
Shop[3]	Defects downgrade these Good or Premium panels to factory seconds	
Note: Hardwood plywood panels typically have one side of A-Premium and a lower grade on the other, such as A-1 or A-2, which are combined designations. [1]Also referred to as Cabinet grade [2]Not an HPMA-certified grade [3]Dealer-determined		

off the log butted up side by side. *Book-matched* uses consecutive slices, too, but every other one is flipped over for a mirror image. A book-matched face resembles the right and left pages of an open book (see match illustration on *page 33, top left*).

Understanding grading

Hardwood plywood grades, set by both the Hardwood Plywood Manufacturers Association (HPMA) and individual mills, cover varying degrees of quality from top of the line to bottom. But you only need to acquaint yourself with those described in the table. All retail outlets carrying hardwood plywood will be familiar with these designations.

While not actually part of the grading standards, the classification of hardwood plywood as either Type I or Type II becomes important to you if your project will be used outside. Most hardwood plywood has Type II adhesive, which creates a somewhat water-resistant bond. For outside applications, you'll have to order hardwood plywood bonded with Type I adhesive. This truly waterproof bond raises the cost of the panel, but for outside durability, it's essential.

Shopping tips

Smart planning and shopping pay off when you buy hardwood plywood. Follow these suggestions to get the most for your money.

• **Select a suitable grade.** If you're building a hutch cabinet, for example, and want to make the back of hardwood plywood, only the side that will face the room needs to be of higher quality. A typical ¼" hutch back would have a "good" grade for the face and a "backing" grade for the back. Cabinet doors, where one side is seen only occasionally, require upgrading—"good" face and a "sound" back.

• **Don't buy more than you need.** Since hardwood plywood is expensive, try to minimize leftovers from a 1×8 sheet—storing them risks gouges, scratches, and moisture damage. Often, your dealer will have half-sheets available for smaller projects. The cost will be higher, but they save money by reducing waste. Sometimes, too, you can buy "shop" grades, which can be high quality with some damage such as broken corners, at significant savings.

• **Inspect before you pay the bill.** Broken or smashed corners can't be repaired. Voids, those sunken or hollow spots in the core, won't hold fasteners. Don't accept anything with portions of the core showing slightly through the veneer (this is caused by excess sanding during manufacture). Imperfections in the ply underlying the veneer often telegraph through as a small rise or dent, and they won't sand away. Veneers also may suffer glue failure, overlap at the joints, or even have spaces between them filled with wood putty. Reject any of these imperfections.

Where can you buy hardwood plywood?

Local lumberyards may have only a limited selection, but they can special-order through their lumber wholesaler. Home centers and hardwood specialty retailers carry hardwood plywood in larger metropolitan areas. Begin shopping by checking listings under "Hardwoods & Veneers" in the Yellow Pages.

Also, school shop suppliers won't sell small amounts to individuals, but you might order through the school or perhaps a local cabinetmaker.

HOW TO JUDGE THE FACE SIDE OF HARDWOOD PLYWOOD

Side A

Naturally, you want the best face to show when building furniture and cabinetry from hardwood veneer plywood. Often, though, the "two-faced" nature of premium grades makes that choice a difficult one.

Only the premium grades of hardwood veneer plywood—AA, A, and A1—pose a problem in selecting the right face for a project. These grades have veneers on both sides that may at first glance look nearly identical (especially AA). However, subtle differences do exist, and choosing the right face can make the difference between a good end product and a superior one. Here's what you need to know.

The three characteristics of face

There's a precept among expert cabinetmakers that says a project must be striking from afar and look even better up close. That's why they select the "showing" side of panels according to *color* first, *grain* second, and *splices* last.

Color is the overall tone of the wood. In most cases you'll want a

Which is the best face? The photos show both sides of a premium-grade oak veneer panel. Side A, *left*, has fewer splices and a consistent grain pattern. It's our choice.

Side B

uniform veneer coloring all across the stock, or across each of several panels. In some species, where industry grading standards accept sapwood as well as heartwood for the veneer, there will be a color variation. Here, you'll want to make sure that the color variation occurs regularly enough to form a recognizable pattern.

Grain, your second consideration, should also be consistent across the face of the panel you select. If you're working with straight-grained, rift-cut white oak, for instance, you wouldn't want a portion of it to show any figure. The selection of matching *flitches,* or strips of veneer that make up the panel face, was made by the manufacturer, but it's up to you to choose the most pleasing effect. Once you have chosen the

grain you want displayed in your project, stick with it wherever possible.

Splices, the faintly visible joints between flitches, should be your last consideration after you have settled on the side with the best color and grain. Only when these butted-up flitch edges interfere with appearance will this choice change priority. When both sides look to be the same, the best face will usually have the fewest number of splices. To find them, scan the panel from left to right across the grain.

Imperfections to eliminate

Despite quality-control standards practiced in the hardwood plywood industry, slight imperfections may slip by the inspectors. These flaws may become the deciding factor in selecting which face to use in your project.

The rare, but not unknown, glue stain from the veneering process should eliminate a side, for instance. Or a depression in a core ply that "telegraphs" through as surface roughness (you can find these depressions by running the palm of your hand slowly over the face veneer). Neither of these imperfections can be sanded out, and they will show up noticeably in the finished product.

What if you can't make up your mind, even after considering variations in color, grain, splices, and imperfections? Try this test: Wipe a light coat of tung or Danish oil on both sides of the panel. The oil tends to enhance and magnify everything, including imperfections and should make the choice all the more obvious.

TEN WINNING WAYS TO WORK WITH PLYWOOD

For all of its virtues—stability, strength, and good looks, to name a few—a sheet of hardwood plywood can present some real challenges to the woodworker. For example, cutting a 4X8' sheet down to size without a lot of rigmarole, or cutting through its thin surface veneer without splintering, can be time-consuming or downright frustrating. And, how do you go about hiding those unsightly edges?

To help you deal with these and other problems peculiar to plywood, we've assembled ten of our best tips and jigs. Now, bring on the plywood!

1. How to show your good side when cutting

Circular saw-blade teeth create few splinters as they enter a veneered surface, but may create a lot of chipout as they exit the workpiece. So, always position your stock as shown.

Position the best face *down* when cutting with a portable circular saw.

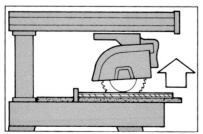

When using a radial-arm saw, position the plywood's best face *up*.

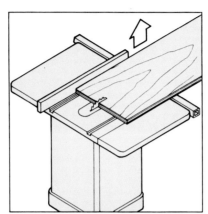

Position the best face *up* when cutting plywood with a tablesaw.

2. Zero-clearance inserts add up to impressive tablesaw results

To minimize splinters on the underside of the workpiece—something that's especially important with a dado blade—make a zero-clearance insert for your tablesaw. Here's how:

Trace the shape of your tablesaw insert onto a piece of ½" plywood (some smaller saws may require ¼" plywood or tempered hardboard). Cut just along the outside of this line, and then sand back to the line.

To cut the zero-clearance slot in the insert, you first have to install a blade that's at least 1" smaller than the largest blade that the saw handles (9" blade in a 10" saw). The outside blades of a stackable dado set work well if you're making the insert for a ⅛"-kerf blade. This is necessary because fully sized blades will interfere with the following steps. If you're making the insert for a dado blade, install the dado blade adjusted to its desired cutting width.

With the saw blade fully lowered, check the fit of the plywood insert. To set the top of the insert flush with the tablesaw top, apply dabs of hotmelt adhesive to each of the insert supports as shown *above right*. Allow these dabs to harden

slightly (5–10 seconds should do it), then install the insert and push it down flush with a straightedge as shown *bottom*. If the insert sinks too low, just pop it off, apply more hotmelt adhesive, and try again.

Now, cover a portion of the insert with your rip fence. *Be careful not to place the rip fence directly above the saw blade.* Slowly raise the blade through the insert as shown *opposite, top left*. With the blade slot cut, remove the insert and replace the smaller blade with a larger one if necessary.

For best results, allow the hotmelt adhesive to cool for 10–15 seconds before putting the insert in place.

Before the hotmelt adhesive cools completely, set the insert flush with the tabletop using a straightedge.

Hold down the insert with your rip fence and slowly raise the blade. *Be careful not to cut into the rip fence!*

In the *WOOD*® magazine shop, we make several insert blanks at once so we have one handy whenever we change blades.

3. A hassle-free way to crosscut long stock on your tablesaw

Crosscutting a long piece of plywood on a tablesaw can be a dangerous—if not impossible—proposition. It doesn't have to be.

Clamp a straightedge onto the bottom of your workpiece and guide the straightedge along the edge of the tablesaw extension as shown *below*. If the extension casting has a rough edge, or protruding bolts, you'll have to add a wooden strip to it for the

straightedge to glide against. If you add such a strip, make it the necessary thickness so the blade-to-straightedge distance is a round number.

4. Two ways to gain the upper hand on glue squeeze-out

Glue squeeze-out can do a real number on your finish if allowed to seal the surface of the wood. Unfortunately, these blemishes usually only reveal themselves after you apply a finish. We use two substances—oil and masking tape—to block squeeze-out from coming in contact with the wood.

As shown at the top of *page 39*, you should first apply the masking tape to surfaces adjoining the dado. Then, dry-fit the mating piece into the dado, and apply tape to the

exposed surfaces of this piece. Separate the two pieces, apply glue, clamp, and allow the squeeze-out to form a tough skin before gently peeling away the tape.

Masking tape may not stick to all woods, so we occasionally use Watco natural oil as shown at the bottom of *page 41*. First, dry-fit the adjoining pieces, wipe oil where the squeeze-out will occur, separate the pieces, and glue them together. With a sharp chisel, carefully shave away the glue squeeze-out after a tough skin forms.

Before using this method, test the oil's compatibility with the finish you will apply over it. The oil will blend nicely with most stains, but may discolor a clear-finished piece.

5. How to cut plywood with a portable circular saw or router

Many of us don't have tablesaws or workshops large enough for ripping full sheets of plywood. What we need: a system for getting good results with portable tools. You can use a router for smooth cross-grain cuts, or a portable circular saw for fast ripping. The edge guide shown on *page 38, top right* accommodates both tools. (You can make the guide for use with just one tool, as we did with the guide shown *above* and in the photo on *page 38, bottom*.)

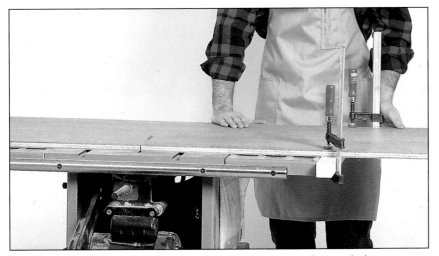

A straightedge clamped to the bottom side of your workpiece helps you crosscut long panels quickly, easily, and accurately.

continued

TEN WINNING WAYS TO WORK WITH PLYWOOD
continued

Make the ¼" base wide enough so you can trim one side to width with your router as shown in the drawing at *right center* and the other side with your saw. This way, the router bit or saw blade trims the ¼" base so you can align this edge with the marks on your workpiece for quick, precise results. We made our edge guide 8' long so it handles almost any plywood job.

You must use the same saw and blade, and the same router and bit, with the guide at all times, so it helps to write the make and size of these tools on each side of the guide. Otherwise, the edges of the guides will not align with your cutoff marks as required in the following step.

To make a cut, line up either of the trimmed base edges with your cutoff marks, clamp the edge guide in place, and cut away. As shown in the photo *below,* we prefer to support the workpiece on top of several 2×2s resting on top of sawhorses.

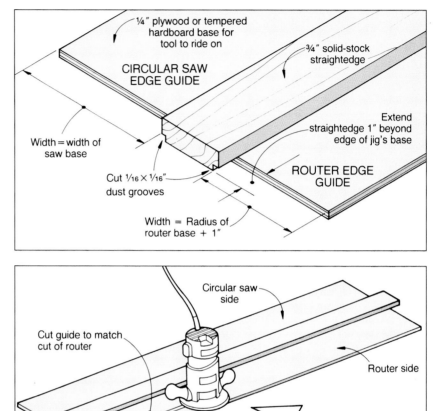

¼" plywood or tempered hardboard base for tool to ride on

¾" solid-stock straightedge

CIRCULAR SAW EDGE GUIDE

Width = width of saw base

Cut ¹⁄₁₆ × ¹⁄₁₆" dust grooves

Width = Radius of router base + 1"

Extend straightedge 1" beyond edge of jig's base

ROUTER EDGE GUIDE

Circular saw side

Cut guide to match cut of router

Router side

Use several 2×2s to make an inexpensive support that prevents you from cutting into your sawhorses.

6. How to get the edge on plywood

Plywood components such as shelves require edging of some sort, and we prefer solid wood over edge banding because of its durability and natural look.

First, glue a ¼"-thick strip of wood onto the edge and trim it as shown at *right*. If you want the edge to look as inconspicuous as possible, trim it to 1⁄16" thickness as shown at *far right*.

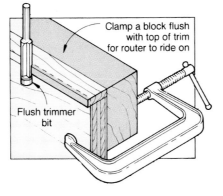

Clamp a block flush with top of trim for router to ride on

Flush trimmer bit

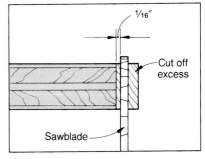

1⁄16"

Cut off excess

Sawblade

7. Getting cornered was never easier

Like edges, plywood corners need disguising. Here's how to handle rabbeted and mitered corners.

For rabbeted corners, glue a 5⁄16"-thick trim piece onto the edge of one of the workpieces, and follow the sequence at *right*.

When faced with a mitered corner, we insert a ⅛" spline for increased strength as shown *below, left* and *center*. If the corner doesn't align perfectly, add a 1⁄16"×1⁄16" strip as shown in the Detail drawing *below right*. Sand the strip smooth with the surface.

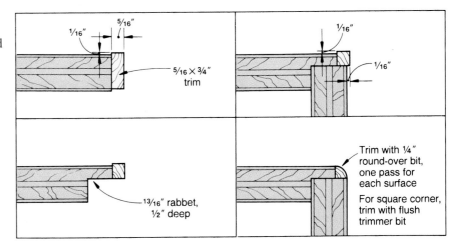

1⁄16"   5⁄16"

5⁄16 × ¾" trim

1⁄16"   1⁄16"

13⁄16" rabbet, ½" deep

Trim with ¼" round-over bit, one pass for each surface

For square corner, trim with flush trimmer bit

continued

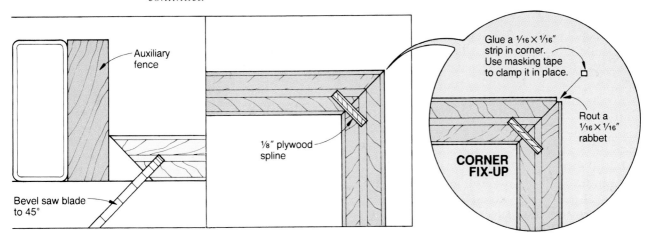

Auxiliary fence

Bevel saw blade to 45°

⅛" plywood spline

Glue a 1⁄16 × 1⁄16" strip in corner. Use masking tape to clamp it in place.

Rout a 1⁄16 × 1⁄16" rabbet

CORNER FIX-UP

TEN WINNING WAYS TO WORK WITH PLYWOOD
continued

8. To cut dadoes with a router, you need this jig

Routers equipped with straight or spiral bits cut clean dadoes but have one drawback: you can't adjust the bit for different cutting widths. Until now.

With the jig shown *below,* your router, and a single straight bit, you can cut dadoes in widths that range from your bit's width to twice your bit's width. For example, with a ½" bit you can cut dadoes from ½" to 1" wide.

With this jig you can rout tight-fitting dadoes every time.

To build the jig, see the drawings and Bill of Materials at *right* and *opposite.* We sized this jig for routers with 6" bases. If your router has a larger or smaller base, you'll need to change the length of Parts B accordingly. The jig will handle stock up to 25" wide, but you can make Parts A and D longer for larger workpieces.

To use the jig, adjust Part D so it's parallel to Part A and separated from Part A by the width of the router base (place the router base on top of Parts B to make this adjustment). Turn the carriage bolts mounted in parts C counterclockwise until they contact Part D.

Now, turn the carriage bolts clockwise as many revolutions as necessary (each revolution equals ¹⁄₁₆") to make up the difference between the width of the straight bit and the width of dado you

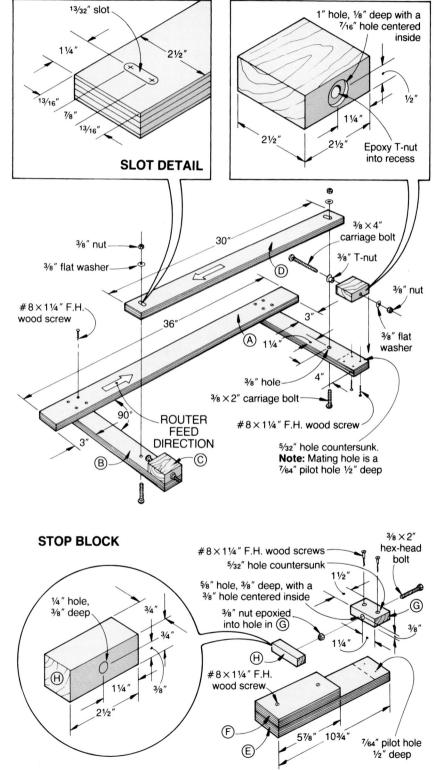

SLOT DETAIL

STOP BLOCK

Bill of Materials

Part	Finished Size		Mat.	Qty.
	T	W	L	
A	¾"	2½"	36"	P	1
B	¾"	2½"	14⅜"	P	2
C	1¹⁄₁₆"	2½"	2½"	S	2
D	¾"	2½"	30"	P	1
E	¾"	2½"	10¾"	P	1
F	¾"	2½"	5⅞"	P	1
G	¾"	1½	2½"	S	1
H	¾"	¾"	2½"	S	1

Material Key: P—Plywood, S—Solid stock

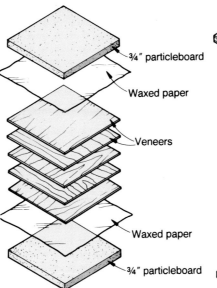

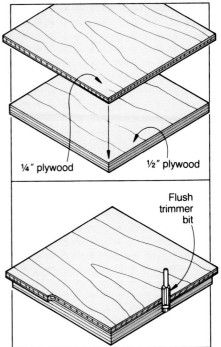

need. For example, if you need a ¾" dado, and have a ½"-diameter straight bit in your router, back away the carriage bolts ¼" (four revolutions). Mark the carriage-bolt head with a single dot near its rim so you can keep track of the number of revolutions. Now, lock down Part D by tightening the nuts that hold it.

For a tight-fitting dado, test your adjustments by making some cuts in scrap stock. Clamp the jig to the scrap stock and feed the router along part A in the direction indicated by the arrows on the jig. After completing this cut, feed the router along Part D in the opposite direction. As you enter and exit the cuts, the bit will also cut dadoes in Parts B. This won't harm the jig, so long as you don't make cuts deeper than ⅜". If you make a deep cut, replace Parts B.

To cut stopped dadoes as we're doing in the photo *opposite,* just secure the stop block in place by turning its hex-head bolt.

9. Thin pieces with strength and good looks

Some workpieces—such as fine toy parts or scrollsawed ornaments—have to be thin (¼" or less) *and* strong. The problem: Solid stock won't hold up, and you might not be able to find plywoods in the necessary thickness or species. Even if you can find the right plywood, it's likely to have an inner ply of a contrasting wood. Yuck!

The solution: Cross-laminate several layers of veneer of the same species as shown *above.* Apply an even layer of white woodworker's glue between the veneers and secure the sandwich with clamps. After drying overnight, your homemade stock will have strength *and* good looks.

10. Homemade plywood looks great on cabinetry

The next time you need ¾" plywood with only one good hard-wood face, consider laminating ¼"-thick hardwood plywood to a substrate of fir plywood or particleboard. Why? The cost of these materials (plus the necessary glue) usually amounts to less than the cost of a sheet of ¾" hardwood plywood of the same square footage. And, in our trips to lumber outlets, we've often found ¼" plywood (especially oak) that looks far better than what's available in ¾" plywood of the same species.

As shown *above,* you can make your own plywood by laminating a slightly oversized sheet of ¼" plywood to a substrate (contact adhesive or woodworker's glue will do it). Then, straighten the edges with a flush trimmer bit in your router.

HOW TO SUCCEED AT AIR-DRYING LUMBER

If you're thinking about seasoning your own stock, there's a lot to know before you begin. But in the end, it's how you build the stack that really counts.

Many woodworkers prefer air-dried stock to the kiln-dried variety because they say it works easier and offers truer color. Then, there's the money savings.

Air-drying your own stock can save you at least 50 percent over kiln-dried boards from your lumber retailer. But, doing it yourself does require time, effort, know-how, and the room for stacking and storing. To help you avoid the mistakes that result in firewood, we contacted an experienced, hands-on expert. (See also "What you need to know about drying wood," *opposite*.)

Green wood, wet wood—but not all the same

Robert McGuffy has headed up the wood-drying sequence at the

For an accurate reading with an electronic moisture meter, push the meter's probes into the wood at the center of the board, not at the edge or end.

Anderson-Tully Company's Vicksburg, Mississippi, hardwood-processing facility for decades. At this complex, the largest of its kind in the U.S., Robert has the responsibility for air-drying, and then kiln-drying, about 70 million board feet of hardwood every year. And it's a mix that includes 65 species—all coming to him in varying degrees of wetness.

"Southern species, when you first cut 'em, are different in how much moisture they have," Robert says. "Take white ash, for instance. It has about a 60 percent moisture content. Cottonwood and willow will run 180 percent. Red oak runs 80–90 percent."

Note: *The degree of wetness in wood is called moisture content, and it's expressed as a percentage. But that percentage can often exceed 100 because it represents the ratio of the weight of the water in a piece of wood to the weight of the same wood when it is completely dry. For example, a piece of green wood weighs 50 lbs.; dry, it weighs 20 lbs. That means that the green wood contained 30 lbs. of moisture, or 30/20ths of its dry weight was water. As a percentage (30 divided by 20 equals 1.5), that's a moisture content of 150 percent!*

Such a variance, of course, means that each species—even where you live—requires either less or more time to dry down to the

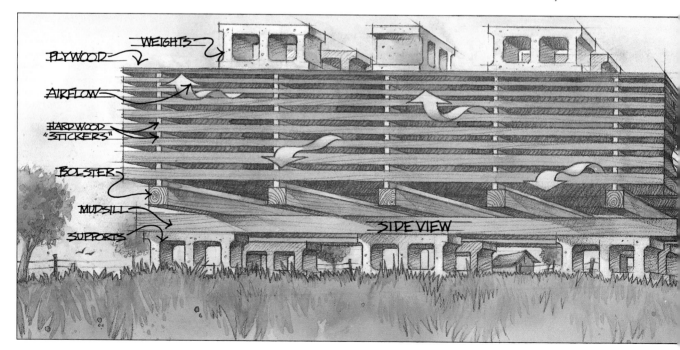

SIDE VIEW

WEIGHTS
PLYWOOD
AIRFLOW
HARDWOOD "STICKERS"
BOLSTER
MUDSILL
SUPPORTS

desired moisture content. At Anderson-Tully, the goal is to air-dry the boards to a 25 percent moisture content. Then, they're ready for the kiln where they'll be reduced to about 8 percent.

Without a kiln, you should try to achieve an air-dry moisture content of 15–20 percent. Further moisture reduction occurs when you move the boards indoors where they'll eventually reach their equilibrium moisture content (EMC).

Note: *The EMC equals a point where the wood neither takes on nor loses moisture due to the atmosphere.*

According to the U.S. Forest Service's Forest Products Laboratory in Madison, Wisconsin, it takes 1"-thick green boards from 45 to 60 days to air dry to 15–20 percent moisture content in sunny, temperate, not-too-humid weather. If you live where it's colder and damper, count on more time. Inside, the drying process can prove slower, taking three or four months before the wood reaches its EMC and can be worked. But achieving workable stock means starting with a proper stack.

Site your stack, then build it right

Pick a storage spot for your boards that's in the open, but avoid low, damp, or boggy areas. And, keep the stack from under trees that can litter it with twigs and leaves. On the other hand, don't pick the sunniest spot in your yard—your boards might dry too rapidly. Keep wind direction in mind, too. Says the experienced Robert McGuffy: "The [prevailing] wind should blow through the side of the stack, not through an end. It'll dry much quicker going through the side, and you won't get end-checks."

At Anderson-Tully, Robert takes extra precaution so the green boards won't degrade in the drying process. "We dip them in an anti-stain sealer, and then put them on stickers [strips of wood that separate the board layers]," he says. "And we seal the ends."

Home woodworkers can do practically the same thing, notes Robert. "Paint the ends of all boards with latex paint [or a commercial sealant such as Sealtite 60 or Mobilicer-M]. Or, put double side-by-side stickers under them. The

check won't go past that second stick. We make our stickers out of most any soft wood [meaning soft hardwood]: poplar, cottonwood, any low-grade lumber," Robert explains. "But I wouldn't make any out of walnut—that stains. The species of the stickers doesn't make that much difference, as long as you make them all the same size. Ours are ripped to 1⅛" wide from boards dressed to ⅞" thick. If the thickness varies, even a little bit, you'll have wavy boards."

Figure on cutting enough stickers per board course to lay them every 2' along the length of the boards. Determine the length of the stickers by estimating the width of the stack you intend to make. Once you cut the stickers, begin stacking the boards as shown *below left.*

What you need to know about drying wood

Drying your own wood can be great, if you follow this advice:

• Be sure to level the stack's foundation, but provide for a slight drainage slope. Put down a vapor barrier if the ground seems damp.

• Select only straight-grained, defect-free boards no thicker than 2" and less than 12" wide.

• Check the stack occasionally. Stains or mildew signal drying too slowly. Excessive checking means drying too fast.

• A moisture meter (about $100 at woodworking suppliers), as shown *opposite top,* is the most reliable means of determining moisture content. Check the wood every few weeks outdoors and after moving it indoors.

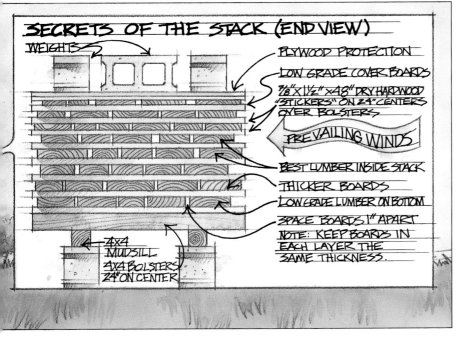

SECRETS OF THE STACK (END VIEW)

WEIGHTS

PLYWOOD PROTECTION

LOW GRADE COVER BOARDS

⅞" X 1½" X 48" DRY HARDWOOD "STICKERS" ON 24" CENTERS OVER BOLSTERS

PREVAILING WINDS

BEST LUMBER INSIDE STACK

THICKER BOARDS

LOW GRADE LUMBER ON BOTTOM

SPACE BOARDS 1" APART

NOTE: KEEP BOARDS IN EACH LAYER THE SAME THICKNESS.

4x4 MUDSILL

4x4 BOLSTERS 24" ON CENTER

THE WORLD OF WOOD: YOUR SPECIES SELECTOR

From Aspen to Yellow Birch, and growing from Maine to Hawaii—and beyond, here is a thorough guide to the world's most popular woods.

RAINFOREST UPDATE

Woodworkers, environmental groups, and businesses aren't just talking about the problems facing the world's rain forests—they're acting. Here's the current status on endangered woods.

Some wood producers get with the program

Concern for the future of the rain forests, particularly those in Brazil's Amazon region, leads many home woodworkers and professionals (as well as buyers of hand-crafted articles) to suddenly question the sources of their stock. They ask, "If I use tropical wood, am I responsible for rain forest destruction?"

Fortunately, some tropical wood producers do treat the forest, and the environment, responsibly. And at last, programs have emerged for identifying these sources and certifying their products so that wood consumers can buy with conscience.

The first such effort, called Smart Wood, hails from The Rainforest Alliance, a nonprofit group based in New York. Smart Wood's criteria includes environmental responsibility (such as watershed protection), sustained yield production, and the positive impact the logging activity has on the local community. For a current Smart Wood list, contact: The Rainforest Alliance, 65 Bleecker St., New York, NY 10012, or call 212-677-1900.

A second program comes from Green Cross Certification Company of Oakland, California, which already has made a name for itself in the ecological certification field. More than 60 manufacturers have had their product claims verified by Green Cross. Now, Green Cross has announced the first wood-product manufacturer to seek certification, the Knoll Group, a leader in office furnishings and a division of Westinghouse Electric.

To attain Green Cross certification, the Knoll Group first must identify their specific tropical timber sources as well as their sources for cherry and oak from temperate forest areas. Green Cross will investigate the sources, grade them ecologically, and develop standards for rating. For more information, write: Green Cross Certification Co., 1611 Telegraph Ave., Ste. 1111, Oakland, CA 94612-2113.

Good Wood

Oregonian John Shipstad, a professional woodworker and board member of the Woodworkers Alliance for Rainforest Protection (WARP) updates a list of tropical wood producers and retailers of their wood in order to inform concerned woodworkers of environmentally responsible sources. At press time, John's "Good Wood" contact sheet cited 16 producers, importers, and retailers. Among the retailers in the U.S. are: Gilmer Wood Co., Portland, OR; Woodworkers Supply, Phoenix, AZ; Pittsford Lumber, Pittsford, NY; Hand loggers Hardwood, Larkspur, CA; and Edensaw Woods, Ltd., Port Townsend, WA.

For a Good Wood list send a self-addressed, stamped, business-sized envelope to: John Shipstad, WARP, 1 Cottage St., Easthampton, MA 01027. To join WARP, enclose a $20 check (made out to Warp) for the annual dues.

Don't use these woods—they're in trouble

The Rainforest Alliance's Tropical Timber Project has compiled a list of endangered woods (*below, left*), and recommends substituting other woods. *WOOD®* magazine endorses that advice.

Afrormosia African mahogany Ebony Iroko Padauk Rosewood

ASPEN

Abundant, blonde, and splinter-free

Aspen, due to sheer quantity alone, supports much of the logging industry across the Great Lakes states and Canada. Abundant because it propagates and grows rapidly in areas cleared by fire or harvest, aspen has many commercial uses. You'll find it in furniture, toothpicks, matchsticks, boxes and crates, paneling, and chipboard. And, this plentiful tree has been a popular source for paper pulp since the late 1940s.

Beavers love aspen bark and consider it a staple food These busy creatures, forever dam-building, also favor the wood for construction. They'll often gnaw down trees a half-mile or more from their damsite, then drag or float them home. Grouse, too, cherish aspen, but for its succulent seeds—so small that it takes over two million to make a pound.

Wood identification

Quaking aspen *(Populus tremuloides),* so-called because its leaves flutter in the slightest breeze, has an unbelievably wide growing range. It grows in a mostly northern belt stretching from Labrador and Newfoundland to Alaska's Yukon River. But, you can even find it in Mexico and Tennessee. Bigtooth (or large-tooth) aspen *(Populus grandidentata),* which also quakes, prefers the Great Lakes states and New England.

Kin to willow and cottonwood, aspen rarely exceeds 60' heights

Big-toothed aspen (*left*), Quaking aspen (*right*)

Aspen sapwood

Aspen streaked heartwood

and diameters of 20". In their first 20 to 30 years they grow rapidly, and quickly renew a forest.

Bark on young trees may be white or greenish white, with dark gray or black welts and ridges. On older trees the bark can be 2" thick, black near the base, and deeply fissured. If you confuse aspen's bark with that of white birch, the leaves provide identification. Both aspen have oval-shaped leaves with toothed edges and stems flattened on the sides.

Sapwood comprises the majority of wood in aspen. It has the whiteness of holly or poplar. The small heartwood core produces light brown wood, often streaked and discolored. It weighs 25 pounds per cubic foot.

Fine-grained, straight, and uniform in texture, aspen generally lacks distinct pattern. Occasional mottle- and stripe-figured logs become veneers.

Working properties

Aspen doesn't contain resin, and has toughness as well as exceptional stiffness. The wood resists splitting in nailing or screwing, yet you can work it easily with hand tools due to its softness. It also glues well.

Due to the tendency for aspen's wood fibers to fuzz when worked, you need to use tools with sharp blades and cutters. While this wood takes paint readily, it blotches when stained unless you first apply a sealer.

You'll find aspen a stable wood that wears without splintering.

However, in conditions favoring decay, it deteriorates.

Uses in woodworking

For carving, aspen makes a first-rate substitute for basswood. You also can fashion it into light-duty furniture, solid paneling, and millwork.

Aspen has no odor and imparts no taste to foodstuffs, so it's ideal for baskets, bowls, and containers. Children's toys made from aspen remain splinter-free.

Cost and availability

Across the southern reaches of the nation, aspen lumber may be hard to find. Where sold, however, the boards will be high quality, but generally neither unusually wide nor thicker than 1". Expect to pay about $1.15 per board foot for lumber and around 50 cents per square foot for mottle- and stripe-figured veneer.

Shop-tested techniques that always work

• For stability in use, always work wood with a maximum moisture content of 8 percent.

• Feed straight-grained wood into planer knives at a 90° angle. To avoid tearing, feed wood with figured or twisted grain at a slight angle (about 15°), and take shallow cuts of about $\frac{1}{32}$ ".

• For clean cuts, rip with a rip-profile blade with 24–32 teeth. Smooth crosscutting requires about a 40-tooth blade.

• Avoid drilling with twist drills. They tend to wander and cause breakout. Use a backing board under the workpiece.

• Drill pilot holes for screws.

• Rout with sharp, preferably carbide-tipped, bits and take shallow passes to avoid burning.

• Carving hardwoods generally means shallow gouge bevels—15° to 20°—and shallow cuts.

BALD CYPRESS

Resistance to decay makes even the smaller, second-growth bald cypress ideal for outdoor construction. Yet, its attractiveness lends itself to indoor projects, too.

Wood identification

The bald cypress (*Taxodium distichum),* classified as a conifer, acts like a hardwood by turning brown or golden in the fall before dropping its needles. Immature trees form a conical shape, have thin, light brown bark, and look much like any other conifer. As a bald cypress ages, however, it begins to more closely resemble a hardwood

Its trunk tapers and develops broad supports called *buttresses* at the base. The bark turns reddish brown, becomes deeply ridged, and peels. At maturity, bald cypress trees have large, uplifting branches forming a broad, irregular canopy.

Bald cypress prefers wet feet, and grows well in damp bottomlands and swamps from Delaware to south Florida, and along the Gulf coast into Texas. Northward, it hugs river valleys through Oklahoma and Arkansas, and up into Illinois and Indiana.

In swampy areas, bald cypress grows in stands. To help anchor the tree in a fragile bottom, its roots develop abovewater shoots or knees for support. On drier ground,

The enduring beauty of the bayou

A cousin to the huge redwood and giant sequoia, the bald cypress easily ranks as the largest and longest living tree east of the Mississippi. Thousand-year-old, first-growth trees attain 150' heights and diameters of 12'. In fact, bald cypress of this size have yielded 100,000 board feet of lumber per acre! However, typical stands average no more than 10,000 board feet.

Today, such huge, ancient trees are a rare find. Loggers locate some by probing the bottoms of swamps. These still-sound prizes—sunk long ago by clearing or storm—must be dredged from the water, then airlifted to the sawmill.

bald cypress mixes with hardwood species.

The wood weighs a bit less than walnut at 28 pounds per cubic foot dry. It has a yellow to pale-brown to reddish hue, and sometimes attractive figure. Bald cypress also feels slightly greasy or waxy. Heartwood has a peculiar, unpleasant odor.

Working properties

Bald cypress wood rates as moderately hard, strong, and stable, with straight, close grain. Although fairly light, the wood holds nails and screws well. It also feels resinous, but this does not affect gluing.

Bald cypress sapwood

Bald cypress works easily with both hand and power tools. And, the wood sands smoothly and grabs on to finishes quite tenaciously.

Bald cypress heartwood

Uses in woodworking

You can use bald cypress successfully for both indoor and outdoor projects. It works for furniture, paneling, cabinets, doors, windows, siding, decking, and trim. Boat-builders find bald cypress excellent for planking, and farmers use it for barn boards, water troughs, and fences.

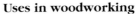

Cost and availability

In the South and southeastern United States, you'll find bald cypress at lumberyards. In other areas availability will be limited due to high shipping cost and the competition from western red cedar. Where you find it, bald cypress will cost about $1.50 per board foot. *Faux satine crotch,* a scarce veneer made from bald cypress crotch wood, occasionally shows up for commercial use in fine-furniture pieces and wall paneling.

BASSWOOD

"How sweet it is!" agree carvers and honeybees

Today's carvers rate basswood highly, but it was probably the Iroquois Indians who first discovered this wood's adaptability to the knife. America's settlers found Native Americans carving ceremonial masks on living basswood trees, then splitting them off from the trunk for hollowing. In the process the Indians saved the innermost bark fibers for fishnets, mats, and cord.

Basswood, also called linden in Europe and parts of the U.S., provides more than quality carving wood, however. Oil from the blossoms of a European variety are an ingredient in perfume, while in America, honey from basswood's sweet flower nectar tingles taste buds. Even the boxes used to ship honeycomb are made of basswood because it imparts neither odor nor taste.

And, if you've ever picked berries in little baskets or received a free wooden yardstick from a lumberyard or hardware store, you probably unknowingly became acquainted with basswood, the source of many of these items.

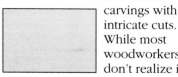

Wood identification

Among the several basswood species in North America, only *Tilia americana* is commercially important and desirable for woodworking and carving. It grows from Maine to South Dakota and southward through Tennessee and northern Texas. But the Lake Superior area boasts the largest concentration of marketable timber.

A symmetrical tree, basswood reaches heights of 90' and has distinctive, large, heart-shaped leaves that make it a favorite for city shade plantings. The largest trees grow in the wild, along stream banks. In June and July, white flowers decorate its branches.

Older specimens have deeply ridged, dark gray bark about 1" thick. The bark of young trees appears lighter in color, smoother, and thinner.

The wood's color ranges from white to creamy white, often containing brown when taken near the center of the tree. Sometimes the wood has bluish mineral streaks, which many find objectionable.

Light in weight at 26 pounds per cubic foot dry, basswood has fine, consistent grain, yet you can dent it with your fingernail. Stable when dry, it shrinks considerably during seasoning.

Working properties

As a carving wood, basswood ranks premier because it won't easily chip or break off ahead of the knife—attributes more apparent in slow-growing northern stock. You'll have no difficulty working basswood with hand or power tools; it sands, glues, and accepts paint exceptionally well. Its fine grain and fibrous cell structure make it hard to stain.

Uses in woodworking

Because basswood holds detail without splitting or breaking, carvers find it perfect for relief work, caricatures, and other carvings with intricate cuts. While most woodworkers don't realize it, basswood can be used for drawer construction, hidden furniture parts, and as a substrate for veneering. It also turns quite well.

Preferred white basswood

Brown-tinted basswood

Parents looking for a wood easy for children to work should consider basswood, since it drills and finishes so effortlessly.

Carving block

Cost and availability

Generally available at hardwood outlets and through mail order suppliers, basswood costs about $2 per board foot.

Boards may be up to 12" wide and 12' long, but smaller sizes are more prevalent. Carving blocks come in 2" to 4" thicknesses. Veneers are rare.

BEECH

Beautiful, bountiful, bendable . . . and barely known

There's a plentiful, cabinet-quality hardwood—pretty as yellow birch, strong as hard maple, and pliable as ash. But hardly anyone uses it! American beech grows over nearly half the nation, yet it seems you only hear about it from the brewery that touts "beechwood-aged" beer. (Beech, as it turns out, imparts no taste of its own to the brew.)

Long ago, however, English craftsmen turned a European variety of beech to make legs for Windsor chairs. Even the ancient Greeks and Romans worked beech into tables, chairs, and chests.

In this country, beech lags behind other woods in popularity because it takes careful handling during seasoning to avoid checking, warping, shrinking, and discoloration. To avoid the processing expense, beech logs are sold for paper pulp or made into clothespins.

Some beech is used in the furniture industry for framing and bentwood parts. In the cabinet shop, it's made into moldings.

Wood identification

You'll find beech in every hemisphere, yet only one species grows in the U.S., *Fagus grandifolia*. Loosely translated, *fagus* means "to eat," referring to its edible nuts, while *grandifolia* means "large-leafed."

Beech trees often grow in pure stands in lower elevations from Maine south to northern Florida and west to Wisconsin and Texas. In prime conditions, trees may tower to 120' and approach 4' in diameter. A slow grower, beech is a survivor, living up to 300 and 400 years.

You can spot beech by its smooth, skinlike, silver-gray bark, here and there disfigured by dark blotches and scars.

Beech wood resembles yellow birch, but with a tint of red in the darker brown heartwood and a hint of pink in the lighter sapwood. The grain is fine, with telltale, tiny pores. Count on beech to be hard, strong, and heavy—it weighs about 45 pounds per cubic foot dry.

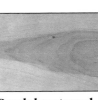

Beech heartwood

Beech sapwood

Working properties

Think of beech as working like hard maple and bending like ash. It doesn't yield easily to hand tools, but it machines well.

Screws and nails hold tight in beech's close grain. Gluing presents no problems, either. The wood readily takes stain and sands to a smooth finish.

Beech does have a peculiarity, however. Because of the heartwood and sapwood's markedly different expansion and contraction rates, you wouldn't mix the two in the same project. If you did, you could end up with separated joints or uneven surfaces in the finished piece.

Uses in woodworking

Beech represents one of a handful of woods that could be classified as "all-purpose" for interior use. It fills the bill for frame construction as well as finished surfaces, and it bends when steamed.

Made into drawers, beech exhibits the unique property of becoming slicker as it rubs against other wood members.

In woodturning, beech excels in objects with delicate stems, such as goblets. For toys, it resists splintering and chipping, and has no toxic properties (keep that quality in mind for bowls and cutting boards, too). Beech also resists wear when wet.

Cost and availability

Although beech may be abundant in the forest, you won't find it everywhere at retail, especially far from its source. The large suppliers that carry beech charge less for it than the more popular hard maple or yellow birch.

Beech boards may be as wide as 12" and range up to 16' long. While beech sometimes becomes veneer, due to lack of demand you'll seldom find it used as the face on hardwood plywood.

BLACK CHERRY

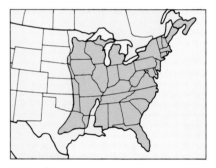

The poor man's mahogany

Although today we think of black cherry as one of the classic furniture woods, it wasn't always that way. Settlers in the Appalachian Mountains, for example, valued the tree's fruit more than its wood. They dubbed the tree "rum cherry" because from its dark purple cherries they brewed a potent liquor. Also, black cherry's inner bark contributed to tonics and cough medicines. Elsewhere, though, the wood was more appreciated.

Early New England furniture makers often found the price of fashionable Honduras mahogany beyond reach and turned instead to native black cherry. Because black cherry wood eventually darkens to a deep reddish brown, these frugal craftsmen mixed what they called "New England mahogany" in with the real thing.

Today, cherry still appears in classic reproductions of colonial-style furniture. It has also climbed in popularity as a new look in kitchen cabinets.

Wood identification

Black cherry *(Prunus serotina)* ranges from the Missouri River east to the Atlantic Ocean, but the species develops best in the Allegheny and Appalachian Mountains of the East. There, in forest conditions, trees grow to 100' heights and 4' diameters.

Young black cherry has satiny, dark, red-brown bark that develops into gray flaky scales as the tree matures. Oval-shaped, pointed leaves appear in the spring. Then, before the new, reddish leaves turn dark green, flowing clusters of white flowers bloom. By late summer, purple, pea-sized cherries appear. Birds eat them and distribute the seeds

The heartwood of black cherry has a light pinkish-brown color when freshly cut. Sunlight deepens it to a dark orange-red. The cream-colored sapwood, however, never darkens to match.

Black cherry's straight, close, and finely textured grain generally

Natural range

features a gently waving figure. Sometimes, trees yield boards with rippled or quilted patterns. Dark spots—actually gum pockets—often appear in black cherry heartwood. Avoid selecting these boards, or at least keep pockets to a minimum.

At 35 pounds per cubic foot, black cherry weighs less than maple. And, it is two-thirds as hard but just as strong and stable.

Uses in woodworking

Rated as a fine cabinet and furniture stock by centuries of craftsmen, black cherry has few limits. It takes abuse as tables, desks, and chairs. Black cherry also becomes musical instruments and architectural paneling, as well as millwork. It's only moderately durable outdoors.

Black cherry with sapwood

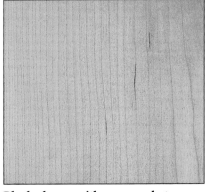

Black cherry with gum pockets

Availability

At about $3 per board foot, black cherry costs approximately the same as red oak. Outlets farther from the source will, of course, charge more. You also can buy black cherry plywood—usually almost twice the price of a sheet of red oak. Plain-sliced veneer costs about 50 cents per square foot; figured veneer runs slightly more. Turning squares, buttons, and plugs also are available.

Machining methods

Select boards with a minimum of sapwood and gum pockets. *Then, remember these tips:*
• Black cherry planes extremely well due to its fine, close grain, but take light cuts in jointing. Dull blades burnish it.
• We've found that for some reason steel blades burn black cherry less than carbide-tipped blades. Avoid burning by feeding the stock without hesitation. In crosscutting, carbide blades outperform steel.
• Except for the common twist drill, any type of bit does well. However, use slower drill press speeds (about 250 rpm). A pause will burn the wood.
• In routing, black cherry doesn't chip or tear like maple, but it will burn during a split-second

hesitation. Take light passes without stopping.
• All types of woodworking adhesives work well, as long as you carefully control squeeze-out. It mars a clear finish more jarringly than on other woods. To check, wipe joints with thinner.
• Because black cherry is nearly as hard as maple, it scratches easily in cross-grain sanding, so never overlap strokes where joints bring the grain together at right angles, such as the corner of a face frame. For best results, use a cabinet scraper to remove scratches between grit changes.
• You probably won't want to stain cherry, except to blend sapwood with darker heartwood. For control, we recommend aniline dye. To hasten cherry's natural tendency to darken, mix a solution of 1 or 2 ounces of sodium hydroxide (lye, poisonous) to a gallon of water, brush it on the wood, then neutralize with water. Experiment for shades.
• Although oil finishes and clear lacquers or varnishes work equally well on cherry, you'll get a smoother finish on this fine-grained wood if you thin the first coat to act as a sealer. Then, sand with 400-grit or 0000 steel wool after it's dry and recoat.

Carving comments

Although hard, black cherry takes detail and finishes beautifully. *For an eye-catching, natural-finish carving, follow these suggestions:*
• Flat-sawed wood has the most grain pattern; quarter-sawed boards (growth rings perpendicular to the width of the board) the least.
• Power-carving tools fit black cherry. Use carbide burrs.
• To remove small scratches on the finished carving, first sand with a coarse sanding drum followed by a fine sanding drum. Then, go over the piece with a coarse sanding disc, using a rocking motion. Hand-sand with 150-grit, then 320-grit.

Turning tricks

Cherry turns nearly effortlessly, as long as you use sharp tools to shear the wood. To sand, shut off the lathe and start with 150-grit, working only with the grain.

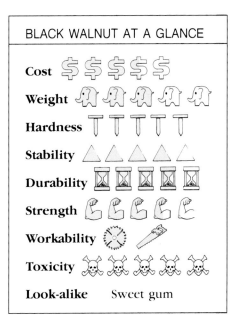

BLACK WALNUT AT A GLANCE

Cost	💲💲💲💲💲
Weight	🐘🐘🐘🐘🐘
Hardness	T T T T T
Stability	△ △ △ △ △
Durability	⬛ ⬛ ⬛ ⬛ ⬛
Strength	💪 💪 💪 💪 💪
Workability	⚙️ 🪚
Toxicity	☠️ ☠️ ☠️ ☠️ ☠️
Look-alike	Sweet gum

BLACK WALNUT

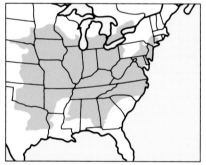

The native aristocrat

Ancient Romans loved walnuts and thought so highly of the meaty fruit that they planted the tree throughout south central Europe and England. Attention always focused on walnut for its nut crop, while oak prevailed as the choice for furniture.

In America, though, native black walnut has always been prime stock. While frontier families gathered walnuts to eat, city craftsmen worked the dark wood into classic pieces. Today, black walnut continues as the aristocrat of native hardwoods and the hallmark of tradition.

Wood identification

European walnut *(Juglans regia)* carries the names of countries and regions, such as English walnut,

French walnut, and Circassian walnut from the Caucasus Mountains along the Black Sea. A walnut *(Juglans neotropica)* also grows in South America.

North America claims two walnuts: white walnut or butternut *(Juglans cinerea),* favored by carvers, and black walnut *(Juglans nigra).* It's black walnut, though, that woodworkers covet.

Black walnut's range covers most of the eastern half of the U.S. and southern Ontario. However, prime walnut requires moist, deep, rich, well-drained soil, such as found in the upper Mississippi River valley.

In idyllic conditions, walnut reaches a height of 150' and a 6' diameter. More commonly, however, it matures at about 100' with a 3' diameter. The tree's thick, dark brown to brownish-gray bark has marked ridges.

Walnut's distinctive leaves measure 1–2' in length and carry a dozen or more leaflets. In spring, flowing catkins emerge on branch twigs. In mid-summer, nuts appear.

Natural range

Walnut's heartwood varies from a purplish-brown with thin, dark veins to gray-brown and even orange-brown. The narrow sapwood tends to be white.

Unfigured walnut has straight, somewhat open grain. Figured walnut—fiddleback, burl, stump, and crotch—feels coarse-textured. A cubic foot of dry walnut weighs about 39 pounds, making it just a little heavier than cherry.

Uses in woodworking

Walnut remains a favorite for furniture, paneling, musical instruments, turned bowls, relief carvings, and sculpture. Veneer proves popular in marquetry and as furniture accents. Walnut's

Straight-grained black walnut

Crotch-figured black walnut

shock-resistance, strength, and stability also make it perfect for shotgun and rifle stocks.

Availability

Selling from coast to coast, walnut ranks as our most expensive native hardwood at a cost of about $4.50 per board foot. It's also offered as plywood, furniture squares, buttons, plugs, turning blocks, and dowels. Plain veneer costs about fifty cents per square foot, but up to $3 for highly figured grades.

Machining methods

Black walnut rates as classic cabinet stock not only because of its eye-appeal, but because you get good results with either hand or power tools. It does, however, sometimes require special treatment. *Our suggestions:*

• Black walnut dust can irritate the eyes, so wear protective goggles, a dust mask, and have adequate ventilation or dust removal.

• Avoid any tearout by taking shallow cuts when jointing. And, try this on the planer: Run two short pieces of stock the same thickness as the walnut board through the planer at the same time—one ahead and one behind. This levels the infeed and outfeed rollers for a chip-free cut.

• In crosscutting, attach a backing board to the miter fence to act as a chip breaker.

• Walnut doesn't burn easily in routing, but shallow passes eliminate tearout.

• Any adhesive performs well with walnut, but in joining with white or yellow glues, keep glue squeeze-out to a minimum and skim off skinned-over glue. Dry glue discolors the dark wood and shows up in the finish. (Elmer's new dark glue minimizes this.)

• Straight-grained walnut generally doesn't require filling. Figured walnut—especially burls and crotch wood—has irregular, more open grain that you should fill.

• Staining walnut isn't necessary, unless color is uneven. Then, aniline dyes won't cloud the grain.

• The best finish for walnut is a clear one. Several coats of Danish oil provide clarity. For protection, add a compatible clear topcoat.

Carving comments

Walnut works best for sculptures and large figures with simple lines, or signs and relief carvings. If you do select walnut for a carving project, remember these tips:

• Deep cuts along the grain may cause the wood to pop out.

• Walnut's grain varies from very open to almost closed, depending on where it grew. Each performs differently. Open-grain walnut carves easier. Closed-grain may be more difficult to but it takes a finer finish.

Turning tricks

Walnut turns best at a lathe speed of 800–1,000 rpm, and requires sharp tools. Bowl turners know that walnut's pronounced end grain in the bottom of a bowl tears easily and produces a rough surface that's difficult to smooth. Here's what Arizona turner John Lea does to counter that:

• Leave a little extra thickness— about ⅛" or less—in the end grain at the bowl's bottom. Then, stop the lathe and with a power disc or flap sander, sand the grain down to a slightly lower level than the surrounding wood. Turn on the lathe and sand the remaining wood around the bottom. This method gives you a round bottom instead of the oval shape you get with the uneven sanding done with the lathe on.

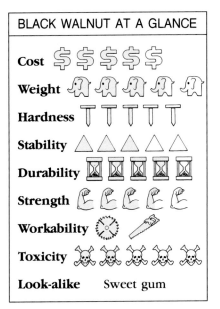

BLACK WALNUT AT A GLANCE				
Cost				
Weight				
Hardness				
Stability				
Durability				
Strength				
Workability				
Toxicity				
Look-alike	Sweet gum			

BLACK WILLOW

Stock for caskets, cricket bats, and wooden legs!

In folklore, the willow represents mourning and lost love. Yet, the wood was said to bring luck at childbirth, and brew from its bark cured aches and pains. Along with hazel and birch, willow was accepted as a top divining wood. A willow fork, held correctly above the ground, would bend to indicate water below.

To ancient Greek and Roman craftsmen, willow was an easily worked utility wood. In England, the willow grew to star status, supplying the stock for cricket bats and polo balls.

Early settlers in the New World began the tradition of using willow for woven baskets, and may have even discovered its usefulness as a switch to tan young bottoms. In the Adirondacks and throughout the East, bark-on willow made popular furniture. And in the South, the wood became casket stock. But it was as artificial limbs that lightweight willow wood really performed, combining softness with superior shock absorbency.

Wood identification

Botanists have identified more than 300 willow species around the world, with more than half of them growing in the eastern U.S. and Canada. All willows, however, have similar characteristics to Black willow (*Salix nigra*), the largest of all willows and the only one of suitable size for commercial lumber.

Because it prefers wet feet, black willow mainly grows in bottomlands along streams and lakes from the Rocky Mountains to the Atlantic Ocean. In the Mississippi Delta region, black willow appears in stands, where it reaches 100' heights with a straight, clear trunk of 3–4' in diameter. Open-grown willow usually attains a height of about 40' and has a crooked trunk (or trunks) with many branches.

The bark of black willow appears dark brown to black, with fissures dividing thick ridges. Its slim branches, covered with narrow blade-like leaves up to 6" long, form a graceful crown.

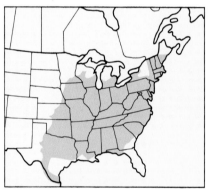

Natural range

At 26 pounds per cubic foot air dry, willow weighs about the same as butternut. The fine-grained, even-textured wood of light-brown color with darker streaks along the grain could pass for yellow poplar. And although willow rates as relatively soft and not structurally strong, it won't readily splinter from a sudden blow.

Uses in woodworking

Even if you're not into crafting cricket bats, you may want to use willow for making toys, boxes, country projects for painting, and even utilitarian furniture. You can weave young willow shoots with the bark on (collected in cool

Willow sapwood

Willow heartwood

months) into baskets or picture frames. Or, carry that further by bending green branches, also with the bark on, into chairs and settees.

Willow, like cottonwood, also carves well. Its texture adapts to turnings, too.

Availability

Hardwood suppliers serving commercial cabinetmakers often carry willow because it sometimes fills in for more costly cabinet woods for drawer sides or unexposed parts. In regions where the tree grows to large sizes, local mills also may offer willow. Expect to pay about $1.75 per board foot for the best grades. You normally won't find willow veneer at retail—it goes for architectural panels.

Willow shares much with cottonwood, including its unfami-

liarity among woodworkers. But as with most secondary species not associated with the cabinet class, willow has many uses at an economical price.

Best be warned, though, willow tends toward woolliness. That is, its fine wood fibers lift from the grain during machining and sanding operations, a feature that adds to finishing time. *But you can work this untouted wood, if you follow this advice:*

Machining methods

• Be sure your stock has been well-seasoned. Thick willow might have pockets of dampness, a condition caused by rushed processing. Feel the wood for cool spots that indicate moisture. Working willow with moisture pockets will result in warpage.

• Sharp cutting edges reduce the chance of fuzziness during planing and sawing. On the jointer, willow's tight, even grain poses no problems.

• Because willow won't easily splinter, it won't tear out when crosscutting. But in ripping, the tight grain requires a rip-set blade with 24 teeth or less.

• Use only use the very sharpest router bits on willow, and take several passes to make the cut. The wood won't burn, but dull bits make it fuzz all the more.

• Don't worry about the predrilling associated with other hardwoods. Because of willow's softness and resistance to splitting, both nails and screws drive without effort. And all glues work equally well.

• Reduce willow's fuzzing during sanding by applying a sealer coat of thinned-down finish after the first once-over with abrasive. Subsequent sandings will produce a satin finish.

• Willow heartwood often displays darker streaks, but don't hesitate to stain because of them. The streaks won't interfere with even coloration. In fact, the wood

accepts both water-based and petroleum based stains equally well. And you can select from any of the available final finishes.

Carving comments

Carve willow for relief or in-the-round with knives, gouges, or power equipment, but keep these points in mind:

• Combat willow's tendency to fuzz with keen cutting edges.

• Because willow doesn't splinter, knives and gouges won't stray in its straight grain. But don't pursue the same intricate detail that basswood allows.

• Willow's lack of figure and normally less-than-interesting grain call for paint or stain.

Turning tricks

Keep turning tools sharp to fight fuzz, but otherwise, willow presents no problems. The wood can even occasionally display exceptional mottled figure that would look particularly interesting on large bowls.

BLACK WILLOW AT A GLANCE					
Cost	$	$	$	$	$
Weight	🦛	🦛	🦛	🦛	🦛
Hardness	T	T	T	T	T
Stability	△	△	△	△	△
Durability	⊠	⊠	⊠	⊠	⊠
Strength	💪	💪	💪	💪	💪
Toxicity	☠	☠	☠	☠	☠
Workability	⚙		🪚		
Look-Alike	Yellow poplar				

BUTTERNUT

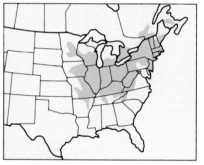

Walnut's kissing cousin

Most all woodworkers have heard of revered and costly black walnut, even if they might not have worked it. On the other hand, butternut—although a walnut, too—remains scarcely recognized as quality stock.

In fact, butternut has more renown as a nut producer than as a woodworking wood. Ever since the pioneer days, people have gathered its sweet, oily nuts with relish each fall. Early Americans also knew butternut as a dye. "Butternut jeans," homespun overalls dyed brown in the juice of butternut husks, were a common sight. And, like the hard maple, the tree was even tapped for its sweet sap, which was processed into syrup.

Historically, though, carvers have always made the most use of butternut as a highly desirable wood. Its straight grain and softness translate into easy carving. For that reason, many intricately carved church altars turn out to be butternut.

Wood identification

Butternut (*Juglans cinerea*), also known as white walnut and oil nut, grows in a northern range from southern New Brunswick in Canada to the North Carolina mountains and west to eastern Minnesota. The tree never appears in stands, but occurs sparsely in rich, moist bottomland soils.

A medium-sized tree, butternut generally grows 30–50' in height and to a trunk diameter of 1–3'. But in prime forest conditions, it can reach 80–100' and diameters of 4'. For instance, the largest butternut on the National Register of Big Trees stands 88' tall.

At a distant glance, butternut resembles black walnut in shape, although it never grows as tall and tends to spread more. And the bark has a gray color instead of the dark brown of black walnut.

The alternate, frondlike leaves are 15–30" long and have as many as 17 pointed leaflets, that on the underside are sticky to the touch. Butternut trees produce oblong nuts with thick, leathery husks and

Natural range

sweet, oily kernels that squirrels love. The nuts drop simultaneously with the leaves in the fall.

Butternut's coarse, straight-grained wood features a light tan color and a beautiful luster. At 27 pounds per cubic foot air dried, butternut weighs less than black walnut. It's also softer, less durable, and not as strong. In stability, the two are equal.

Uses in woodworking

Butternut often becomes carved furniture and mantelpieces, as well as relief, figure, and sculptural carvings. Stained, it imitates walnut in furniture and paneling. Where it's plentiful, the wood becomes cabinets, molding, boxes, and

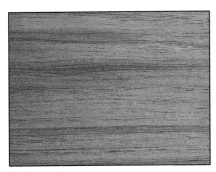

Butternut

crates. Even wormy butternut, which turns up on occasion, may prove worthy for use in certain projects, such as relief carvings or boxes.

Availability

Because today few woodworkers other than carvers demand butternut, and a fungus has infected trees in parts of its range, it may be difficult to obtain except at large hardwood lumber dealers located within its range. But specialty suppliers catering to turners and carvers frequently offer butternut blanks.

When you do find butternut stock, the boards usually won't run extra wide or long due to the lack of large, clear logs. This factor also contributes to butternut's relatively high cost—over $3.00 per board foot for select and better. Butternut veneer or plywood generally isn't available at retail because it is only made for the architectural trade.

Butternut wood sometimes turns out to be wormy, the work of powder-post beetles and their larvae. Such damaged wood can be used for attractive projects, as long as the varmints aren't still working! Kiln-drying usually solves any potential problems, and a thoroughly applied, tough finish guarantees any survivors' demise, but it pays to closely observe all wormy wood for pests before buying.

Machining methods

Butternut works more easily than black walnut with hand and power tools because the wood ranks lower in all strength properties than its cousin. That's a plus, but also a caution. Butternut's softness makes it more susceptible to nicks and dents as you work the wood. And there's more to keep in mind:

• Although black walnut dust can irritate the eyes, butternut doesn't have that tendency. But as with all woods—especially hardwoods—wear a dust mask when doing fine sanding.

• The wood's coarse grain requires care when jointing or planing to avoid tearout. Make several shallow cuts to remove wood instead of one deep one.

• Attach a backing board to the miter fence to act as a chip breaker when crosscutting.

• Butternut, due to its softness, shouldn't burn when routed, but shallow passes eliminate any possible tearout or chipping.

• You won't have any problem gluing butternut—its coarse texture draws in adhesives, ensuring a strong bond.

• Butternut accepts all types of stains (you can even stain it to pass for black walnut) without filling first. But the rich tan wood may look best with a more natural clear finish.

• Although oil finishes prove popular on butternut carvings, you can improve the wood's natural luster by first burnishing it (rubbing the wood with the back of a spoon, gouge, or glass bottle to compact the surface of the fibers for more sheen).

Carving comments

Butternut is a favorite of relief carvers because it takes fine details and finishes to a beautiful luster.

But to avoid warp on large works, edge-join two or three pieces rather than use a single board. Also, keep these other tips in mind:

• In a relief carving, carve the sapwood side of the board to reduce any tendency for it to warp or cup. Look at the growth rings visible in the end to locate the sapwood side. The larger rings will be on what was the outside of the tree.

• Be cautious when taking deep cuts along the straight grain as the wood may pop or tear out.

Turning tricks

The coarse grain of butternut, and its softness, requires sharp tools. For best results, turn butternut at a lathe speed of 800–1,000 rpm.

BUTTERNUT AT A GLANCE

Cost	$ $ $ $ $
Weight	(5 symbols)
Hardness	(5 symbols)
Stability	(5 symbols)
Durability	(5 symbols)
Strength	(5 symbols)
Toxicity	(5 symbols)
Workability	(2 symbols)
Look-Alike	Honey locust

CALIFORNIA LAUREL

Call me myrtle, if you please

Drive along southwest Oregon's coast, and you'll see signs shouting myrtle novelties. In the Coos Bay-Coquille area, a thriving cottage industry has sprung up to produce these wood items. Why tout this wood? For more than 170 years, the California laurel, commonly called myrtle, has been novel.

"The foliage, when bruised, gives out a most powerful, camphor-like scent....I have been obliged to remove from under its shade, the odor being so strong as to occasion violent sneezing," wrote English botanical explorer David Douglas in 1826.

With myrtle causing such a reaction, Oregon shipbuilders of the mid-1800s must have been a noisy lot. They called on the wood extensively for parts that required strength as well as smooth-wearing qualities. Today, turners and other woodworkers prize myrtle for its beauty.

Wood identification

The California laurel *(Umbellularia californica),* and its distant cousin sassafras, represent the only North American species of an entirely tropical genus.

As home range, myrtle settles between the mountains and the Pacific Ocean, from southern Oregon down through California. Myrtle, an evergreen, doesn't mind high, dry, wind-swept environs, but in them, rarely grows larger than bush-size. To attain its finest development, myrtle demands the rich, moist valley soil. There, the tree, swathed in its thick, reddish-brown bark, can attain a 90' height and a 5' diameter.

Marked by green, glossy leaves from 2½" to 4½" long, myrtle trees bear small yellow-green flowers in the spring. Inedible, round, purple berries appear later.

Myrtle has a tan sapwood and close-grained heartwood of a pleasing light-brown color. And, even the plainest boards have some favorable figure, as myrtle develops attractive mottle, bird's-eye, and swirling burls.

Working properties

In hardness, strength, and weight, myrtle compares favorably with oak. Turners favor myrtle because of its tighter grain and ease of sanding.

The same attributes woodturners praise, however, pose difficulties for craftsmen relying only on hand tools. To work myrtle, even power tools should have carbide blades. When planing or routing figured myrtle, expect some tear-out.

You can glue myrtle with all types of adhesives, and screws hold tightly in the wood. And, you won't need sanding sealers or fillers on myrtle's grain, except in figured areas where grain switches. The wood takes stain and all finishes without problems.

Uses in woodworking

Turners prefer highly figured stock, especially burls for bowls, but also make candlesticks, decanters, and other items of myrtle. Cabinetmakers seek veneers of figured myrtle for custom case goods and furniture pieces.

Cost and availability

Where it grows, myrtle will cost from $1.50 to $3.00 per board foot for plain stock. Burls and figured stock command higher prices. Along Oregon's beaches, you can pick up myrtle driftwood for free, or buy it from coastal roadside businesses.

Expect to pay about $2 per square foot for figured burl veneer. You won't find myrtle plywood available anywhere, and lumber only occasionally in other parts of the nation.

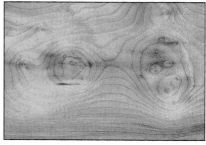

Plain-sawed myrtle

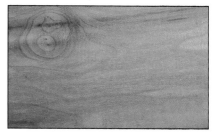

Myrtle burl

CHESTNUT

The pioneers' do-everything wood

Chestnut has a long association with appetites. From the staple made of ground nuts called *polenta* that fed Caesar's legions, to chestnuts roasting by a Yuletide fire, the tree's fame has spread by story and song.

Introduced to northern Europe and Great Britain by the invading Romans, the European variety of the chestnut tree has been cultivated not only for its nuts but for its durable, decay-resistant wood. In the United States, the native American chestnut once dominated the eastern hardwood forests. Growing to a girth greater than most oaks, the chestnut provided the country's pioneers with wood for every imaginable use.

Then, in the early part of this century, a severe blight swept the chestnut, reducing it to a nearly extinct species. Today, the available chestnut lumber and veneer comes from blight victims or from European trees. All the while, experts continue to perfect a disease-resistant strain.

Wood identification

Sighting full-grown chestnut trees in Europe is commonplace. *Castanea sativa,* the European species, remains hearty. In the U.S., the experience could be historic.

However, there's a ray of hope for the American chestnut *(Castanea dentata).* Researchers at the American Chestnut Foundation have found a thriving stand of chestnut trees at an undisclosed site. And, according to a spokesman for the National Arboretum, foresters have discovered a new, harmless strain of the original chestnut blight fungus.

When it reproduced unhampered, American chestnut grew best on the lighter soils in a range from southern Maine to North Carolina, Tennessee, and west to Indiana and Michigan. At maturity, these burly trees stood 60–80' tall and measured 5–6' around the trunk. Deeply furrowed bark formed broad, flat ridges spiraling up the tree.

Early July brought blooms among chestnut's long, thin, toothed leaves, followed by small, prickly burrs. By the end of August, the hard-shelled burrs yielded nuts.

Chestnut has a tiny band of light-colored sapwood. The biscuit-colored heartwood, slightly lighter in weight than maple, resists decay. In color and grain, chestnut strongly resembles oak. Pinworm infestation of the heartwood results in highly valued "wormy" chestnut with tiny holes.

Working properties

Due to its coarseness, chestnut does not turn as well as oak. How-ever, it works easily with other hand and power tools. Lumber from downed wood tends to be brittle, so use fasteners and glue.

You can sand chestnut glass-smooth without difficulty, and the wood responds well to any finish. And, in service, you'll find chestnut one of the most stable woods.

Uses in woodworking

From colonial times, chestnut has been made into anything destined to last: shingles, siding, fence rails and posts, railroad ties, and furniture. It was prized casket stock.

Today, woodworkers select chestnut veneer for custom cabinets, and solid stock for clocks, chests, and furniture. And, antique furniture restorers demand chestnut for replacement parts.

Cost and availability

You can purchase solid (from American and European trees) and wormy chestnut (from American trees) as lumber in up to 3" thickness. However, you'll find it primarily on the East Coast, and in limited quantities. At about $10 per board foot, you'll also pay dearly. More readily available than chestnut lumber, veneer sells for about $4 per square foot.

American chestnut

Wormy chestnut

COCOBOLO

The Central American wood that stands up to a dunking

In the days when merchant ships battled the ravages of South America's treacherous Cape Horn, heavy cocobolo commanded precious little cargo space. But, the opening of the Panama Canal in 1912 changed all that. Cocobolo became common deck cargo, and tons poured into New England ports, where manufacturers turned it into handles on the finest cutlery.

Even though merchants had traded cocobolo for more than 100 years, it was decades before botanists agreed on its name. That's because the tree— first discovered in Panama—was classified as rosewood. Later, botanists found other specimens in Costa Rica, Nicaragua, Honduras, El Salvador, Guatemala, and Mexico, and classified each as a different species!

Such scientific disagreement meant little to manufacturers and craftsmen, however. They knew that the wood was heavy, yet machined easily, could take abuse, and its oil protected it from dunkings in the dishwater.

Wood identification

Cocobolo (*Dahlbergia retusa*) belongs to the same genus as Brazilian rosewood, and in fact, has similar properties. Rosewood, however, likes South America's rain forests. Cocobolo prefers the drier, upland savanna country of Central America's Pacific coast.

A medium-sized—and quite often poorly formed—cocobolo tree reaches a height of only 75–80'. Its reddish brown, scaly trunk measures about 3' in diameter. Amid the tree's large, leathery leaves, tiny yellow blooms flower, then later turn to long, flat seed-pods.

At 65 pounds per cubic foot air dry, cocobolo weighs twice as much as cherry. Not surprisingly, it's too dense to float.

Cocobolo heartwood often carries a sunrise of hues—red, yellow, pink, and black, occasionally streaked with green, purple, and blue. In some boards, a creamy white sapwood borders the colorful heartwood. With age, it darkens.

Working properties

Cocobolo has a bad reputation, but not for its working qualities. This wood is a well-known *sensitizer* that can produce a poison-ivy type rash or other reaction in allergic individuals. If you have an allergy history, work

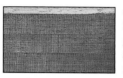
Aged cocobolo

Multicolored cocobolo

cocobolo with full protection: gloves, long sleeves, a dust mask, and protective skin cream.

Dense and hard, cocobolo requires power tools or razor-sharp hand tools. With either, however, edges dull quickly. But, you can almost effortlessly bring the wood to a beautiful luster by sanding and polishing.

Although cocobolo grips screws well, gluing poses a problem. Because of oils and silica in the wood, you should wipe all joining surfaces with lacquer thinner or acetone, then glue immediately. And, we give slow-set epoxy the nod over other adhesives.

Turners often apply only a cabinetmaker's wax to cocobolo. Furniture and case goods require a penetrating oil with a wax topcoat. Other finishes provide only mediocre results.

Uses in woodworking

Tradition typecasts cocobolo as handle stock, but it excels in other starring roles as well. Mirrors, musical instruments (except those that touch the lips), jewelry boxes, clock cases, furniture, bowls, and other turnery all suit it. Remember, though, that the wood darkens with age, and without finish protection, turns nearly black.

Cost and availability

Cocobolo isn't a rare wood. You can buy it for about $18 per board foot. Retailers of exotic wood and mail-order firms usually sell turning squares and blanks, as well as boards and veneer.

DOUGLAS FIR

The globe trotting he-man of American softwoods

Diaries claim that early loggers in what came to be Oregon and Washington often felled 400'-tall trees, each containing enough high-grade lumber to build seven houses! The lofty tree was the Douglas fir, and it still dominates the great forests of the Pacific Northwest.

In 1827, English botanical explorer David Douglas recognized the fir's resource potential. Hoping that the easily grown tree could adapt to his country's reforestation efforts, he shipped seed cones from the Columbia River basin back to the British Isles.

From that introduction, the fir found favor as fast-growing timber first in England, then throughout western Europe. Now, even the adopted habitats of Australia, New Zealand, and South Africa boast Douglas fir forests.

Wood identification

In the U.S., Douglas fir *(Pseudotsuga menziesii)* naturally ranges from the Mexican border north to Alaska, and from the Pacific coast east to the Rocky Mountains. Often found in pure stands, Douglas fir can attain an average mature height of about 300' and diameters from 10' to 17'.

On older trees, the rough bark may be 12" thick. Younger trees have a smooth bark with frequent blisters filled with a pungent resin.

Tiny winged seeds, released from cones as large as a man's fist, quickly germinate in sufficient sunlight. Because of this, Douglas fir quickly takes over and reforests burned or clear-cut areas.

Douglas fir's pinkish-yellow to orange-red heartwood provides a distinct contrast in the growth rings. On flat sawed boards and rotary cut veneer, this translates to an abrupt color change. The thin band of sapwood is often nearly pure white.

Working properties

In comparison to its weight, Douglas fir ranks as the strongest of all American woods. It is also stiff, stable, and relatively decay resistant.

Douglas fir's coarse texture can't easily be worked with hand tools.

And to avoid tearing grain, even power tool blades must be sharp. Yet, the wood grips nails and screws securely, and readily accepts all types of adhesives.

Because Douglas fir contains fewer resins than many other softwoods, count on success with paint and clear finishes. Staining, however, becomes a problem due to the light-to-dark variation between growth rings that causes uneven coloration.

Uses in woodworking

Vast quantities of Douglas fir provide dimension lumber for the construction industry and veneers for plywood. The wood's appearance and easy-working properties have earned it a spot in the manufacturing of windows, doors, and moldings.

Flat sawed, Douglas fir makes attractive, serviceable cabinets and paintable furniture. Sawn as vertical grain, Douglas fir performs well as flooring and looks stunning as cabinetry.

Cost and availability

Found across most of the nation as common construction lumber, Douglas fir falls in the inexpensive price range of about $1 per lineal foot. However, sawed for vertical grain and graded for "superior finish," the cost rises by at least three times. Douglas fir plywood in all grades is readily available.

EASTERN RED CEDAR

Favored for fragrance and flavor

French Acadians, deported from Nova Scotia by the British in 1755 to what is now Louisiana, found a familiar softwood growing in their new land. For its red bark and red wood, they called it *baton rouge,* meaning "red stick," the name the French settlers adopted for their capital city.

Eastern red cedar, the "red stick" of the Acadians, belongs to the juniper family of conifers, one of the oldest on earth. Ancient Egyptians used a juniper to make chariot wheels in 1300 B.C. And the Dutch, who first distilled gin in the 17th century, flavored their concoction with juniper berries, a practice that continues today.

Juniper leaves and twigs also furnish a fragrant oil for medicines and perfume. But moths and buffalo beetles find juniper's sweet smell highly repugnant. That's why eastern red cedar, made into chests and closet linings, has been prized for protecting woolens since colonial times.

When large stands of large trees were abundant, eastern red cedar was used for lead pencils because it shaves so nicely. Now, an African cedar has replaced it as pencil wood, and woodworkers make use of knottier, narrower boards.

Wood identification

Sometimes called red juniper and aromatic red cedar, eastern red cedar (*Juniperus virginiana*) grows from north to south in most of the eastern U.S. and even west into North Dakota and Texas. For soil, it likes every variety except wet, spongy swampland.

Eastern red cedar averages about 16" in diameter and 20' to 50' tall. Rather than the needles typical of evergreens, this tree has lacelike fronds that brown with age. Its bark appears reddish brown and shredded, and easily strips from the trunk. By autumn, eastern red cedar trees develop pale, blue-green berries, much appreciated by birds.

The wood of eastern red cedar is light, weighing about 33 pounds per cubic foot air-dried, and, surprisingly, is 80 percent as strong as white oak. The thin, white sapwood has a pale pink hue, while the heartwood darkens to pinkish red. The oil in the wood causes its pleasant, unmistakable aroma—especially around the knots.

Working properties

Eastern red cedar has a fine grain, but a soft texture. It works

Eastern red cedar with sapwood

Eastern red cedar heartwood

easily with hand or power tools, despite the fact that it is somewhat brittle. In stability, it ranks quite high.

If you want the wood to remain fragrant, don't cover it with a finish. Otherwise, use anything but polyurethane or plastic finishes—oil in the wood makes it difficult for them to adhere.

Note: Unfinished eastern red cedar eventually becomes less fragrant as its oil hardens in the wood surface. You can renew the fragrance by sanding with fine-grit sandpaper. Fresh oil from the inner wood will rise to the surface, renewing the aroma.

Uses in woodworking

Eastern red cedar works well for trim in boats and canoes, as cedar chests, for closet linings, jewelry boxes, bookcases, carvings, and turnings.

Cost and availability

Although it's a softwood, hardwood grading standards apply because eastern red cedar is used primarily as a cabinet wood.

Since clear wood is hard to come by, most eastern red cedar boards carry the "common" grading label, and a fairly inexpensive price of about $1.50 per board foot. Readily available boards rarely exceed 7" widths, 6' lengths, and 1" thicknesses. Veneers, plywood, and particleboard are other products.

EASTERN WHITE PINE

From coins to carpentry, it was colonial America's treasured tree

When the Pilgrims arrived at what was to be called Massachusetts in 1620, stands of tall, stout eastern white pine grew everywhere. In fact, adults could stroll easily beneath them without ducking, since the pines were often branch-free for 40' or more of their 200' height.

Even Captain John Smith noticed more than Pocahontas in the New World, and wrote at length about the great storehouse of trees, not the least of which was the eastern white pine. In fact, this same towering conifer was chosen as the symbol of wealth on the first coin minted in the New World—the Massachusetts Bay Colony's pine-tree shilling.

Once estimated as a resource of some three-quarters of a *trillion* board feet, the eastern white pine became a favorite of New England settlers. They felled the

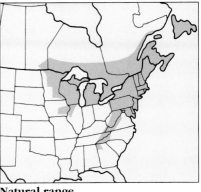
Natural range

trees in great numbers for sailing-ship masts, charcoal, and other items of commerce. But most of the timber went into homes and furnishings.

Wood identification

Second only to California's sugar pine in size among the pines, the eastern white pine *(Pinus strobus),* can, in old forests, reach 230' heights and diameters of nearly 10'. Today, though, white pines grown for lumber rarely reach 100' and a diameter of 2–4' before harvest. Yet, in their natural range from Manitoba to New England and southeastern Georgia, they are the fastest-growing trees, shooting up 18" per year.

The eastern white pine, sometimes called northern white pine and soft pine, prefers deep, sandy-loam soils, but will grow anywhere with sufficient moisture—often in pure stands. With its straight trunk, irregular crown, and horizontally layered branches, you can spot this monarch easily. Up close, look at the 3–5" long, blue-green needles. They're in clusters of five. And the curved, narrow cones can be as long as 8".

The soft, fine-textured, and straight-grained wood of white

pine varies in color from creamy white to red-brown, with little distinction between early wood and late wood. Even with a finish, it mellows with age to a pumpkin color. Light, it weighs about 25 pounds per cubic foot air-dried, but is no stronger than basswood. The least resinous of all pines, eastern white pine remains quite stable while fulfilling many construction and wood-working needs.

Uses in woodworking

As did their pioneer ancestors, today's woodworkers can use eastern white pine for everything from house construction to furniture, carving to millwork, boats to musical instruments. And as "knotty pine," it's a favorite for bookcases and paneling.

continued

EASTERN WHITE PINE
continued

Eastern white pine

Availability

Although the wide, clear boards of yesteryear's woodworking stock are very seldom available today, most wood retailers in the Midwest and East carry eastern white pine. Expect to pay $2 or more per board foot for furniture-grade. As ¾" plywood, its cost can be $60 or more.

It's true that America's settlers relied heavily on eastern white pine—mainly because of the old growth trees' yield of long, wide, clear boards. Today, it's a different story. The biggest, oldest trees were cut long ago, and today's white-pine lumber comes from second-, third-, fourth-, and even fifth-growth stands. This means narrower boards with more knots. So, when you buy white pine:

• Ask for No. 1 Common and Better, or No. 2 Common grades. Similar to hardwood grades, these yield 66⅔ percent and 50 percent clear cuttings respectively (tight knots are allowed).

• Specify only kiln-dried (to 8 percent or less) white pine for your furniture projects. Why? Kiln-drying increases stability and sets the resinous pitch that otherwise can aggravate gluing, or bleed through a finish.

Machining methods

All pines are considered softwoods, but they actually fall into two categories: soft pines and hard pines. White pine lists as a soft pine, and it's easily worked with all hand and power tools. *Keep these tips in mind, however:*

• Eastern white pine has less pitch in its wood than other pines, but gum buildup on cutting edges still occurs. To avoid burning and blade wander from gum buildup when ripping, stop sawing after every 50' or so to clean the saw's teeth with acetone and steel wool or oven cleaner. Better yet, make the switch to a Teflon-coated blade for this wood.

• The wood has little tendency to chip or splinter, so the only precaution necessary in machining white pine is to use a backing board when routing across the grain. If you'll be doing much routing, see the above note about gum buildup.

• Seal all knots in the wood with shellac before finishing to prevent bleed-through.

• When selecting a stain and clear finish, remember that white pine will naturally age darker.

• Even though white pine accepts stains better than most other pines, first use a wash coat of shellac thinned with denatured alcohol to prevent blotchiness.

Carving comments

• The difference in hardness (density) between early wood and late wood is hardly noticeable when carving eastern white pine, a trait that also means that the wood can take fine detail.

• In thick carving stock, though, watch for resin that may bleed through a painted surface. Either let the completed carving season for a few weeks in a warm, dry place, or seal it with shellac before finishing.

Turning tips

• As in carving, thick stock may contain resin canals in which the pitch has not set, and droplets may appear on the freshly turned surface. When dry, the hardened droplets can be scraped off.

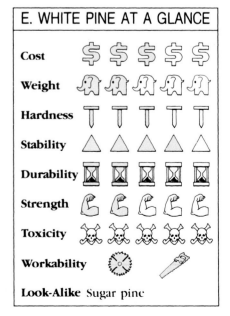

E. WHITE PINE AT A GLANCE				
Cost	$	$	$	$ $
Weight	🐘	🐘	🐘	🐘 🐘
Hardness	⊤	⊤	⊤	⊤ ⊤
Stability	△	△	△	△ △
Durability	⊠	⊠	⊠	⊠ ⊠
Strength	🦴	🦴	🦴	🦴 🦴
Toxicity	☠	☠	☠	☠ ☠
Workability	⚙			🪚
Look-Alike Sugar pine				

ELM

The hard-as-nails hardwood with beauty a burl deep

Throughout history, man has chosen elm when he needed a tough and durable wood. Wheelwrights fashioned wheel hubs from nothing but the rugged elm, then used it to floor long-lasting wagon beds. The Chinese called elm *yümu* and worked it into utilitarian furniture that could take abuse. Fine furniture makers called on elm, too, but in the form of burl veneer from a species growing in Europe's Carpathian Mountains.

In early America, Iroquois Indians tempered fever with a medicine derived from the inner bark of the slippery elm. Years later, players in the new game of baseball chewed this same elm bark to produce a sticky saliva, which when rubbed into the pocket of their glove, made balls easier to catch.

Despite its many uses, elm's primary fame has come from its graceful beauty and the shade it provides. From France to Middle America, elm once lined miles of city streets and country byways. Today, unfortunately, elm trees are being killed by a spreading fungus called "Dutch" elm disease. Efforts to control the disease haven't been successful. Fortunately, the propagation of hybrid, disease-resistant trees shows promise.

Wood identification

Elm claims about 20 species in the temperate regions of the world. The most well known include the stately American elm *(Ulmus americana)* and the slippery elm *(Ulmus rubra)* of the United States, and the English elm *(Ulmus procera)* in Europe and Great Britain.

In the forest, elm often grows 140' tall. But open-grown elms rarely reach that height. Instead, they form a spreading, umbrella-like crown valued for shade.

The English and American elms have deeply fissured bark with crisscrossing ridges of an ash-gray of slippery elm is the same color, but lacks pattern.

You can easily identify elm by its leaves. About 5" long and 3" wide, they have saw-toothed edges ending in a sharp point.

Elm heartwood ranges in tone from reddish brown to light tan, while the sapwood approaches off-white. The usually dramatic grain resembles ash. Moderately dense, elm weighs nearly 40 pounds per cubic foot dry.

American and slippery elm will root practically everywhere east of the Rocky Mountains (except for the high Appalachians and the southern tip of Florida). You'll find elm growing in river bottoms and on low, fertile hills mixed with other species of hardwoods.

Working properties

Hard and tough, elm still bends easily when steamed, and when dry, holds its shape. Its twisted, interlocking grain makes elm difficult to work with anything but power tools. It also won't split

American elm

Slippery elm

Carpathian elm burl veneer

when screwed or nailed, but demands drilling pilot holes. And the wood sands easily to a natural low luster.

Burl veneers tend to be brittle and troublesome to flatten. Try those with flexible backing.

Uses in woodworking

Besides the frequent use of its veneer for paneling, furniture makers take advantage of elm's ruggedness for hidden furniture parts. You'll often find it in chair and sofa frames, backs, and legs. Yet elm's beautiful wood grain also has fine furniture possibilities.

Elm works well, too, for butcher block tops and cutting boards because it has no odor or taste, and it won't split. When in contact with water, elm resists decay, so many boatbuilders use it for planking.

Cost and availability

Today, most elm lumber goes for manufacturing use and very little finds its way to retail outlets. Where you do find it— usually at small, local sawmills—it costs less than $2 a board foot compared to nearly twice that for oak and walnut. Native elm veneer sells for about $1 per square foot—Carpathian elm burl about double that.

HEMLOCK

The softwood that toughens up with age

In the last century, the bark of hemlock was sometimes worth more than the wood. The leather-tanning and fur-processing industries demanded hemlock bark for its high tannic acid content. Hides and skins infused with a tannic acid solution become soft and strong. Tragically, stands of hemlock in the eastern United States and Canada were stripped of their bark, then left on the stump to die.

It wasn't until the '40s boom in wood-frame house construction that hemlock came into its own as lumber. And then, the eastern hemlock's West Coast cousin provided the raw material. Today, hemlock lumber from Oregon, Washington, and British Columbia (where the species represents 60 percent of the mature coastal forest) feeds home construction and millwork manufacturers. Hemlock even gives some hardwoods a run for their money as a lower-cost, yet strong, easy-to-work furniture

stock. In fact, this softwood actually grows harder with age!

Wood identification

Botanist Stephen L. Endlicher christened hemlock in 1847 with the genus name *tsuga*. The Japanese word means "yew-leafed," referring its short, flat, and contrary to legend, poisonous needles.

Eastern hemlock *(Tsuga canadensis)* plants its roots from Canada south to Georgia and west across the Great Lakes states to Minnesota. Western hemlock *(Tsuga heterophylla)*, sometimes called Pacific hemlock, thrives in the moist coastal ranges from Alaska to northern California, but also climbs mountain slopes in Idaho and Montana.

Growing to greater size than its eastern relative—which only becomes 80' tall and 36" in diameter in 250 years—western hemlock represents one of the lumber industry's few remaining sources of large, clear timber. Trees 100 years old can be 150' tall, with a 24" diameter.

The bark of both hemlock species appears cinnamon-red to brown in color and has broad, deep ridges. Seed-bearing brown cones sprout at the ends of branch shoots.

Little color variance between hemlock's heartwood and sapwood results in a nearly uniform buff color in both species. The wood of western hemlock weighs more (about 29 pounds per cubic foot, dry) than that of its eastern relative. Western hemlock also is harder, stronger, straighter-grained, and resin-free.

Working properties

You can work hemlock easily with hand or power tools. In crosscutting, however, expect some tearout.

Western hemlock

The wood grips screws and accepts all glues without a problem. Western hemlock, with its straight grain and finer texture, sands to a silky, reflective smoothness. Because the western variety is resin-free, it accepts any paint, stain, or clear finish with more satisfying results than the eastern species. Don't use either hemlock species outdoors without preservative treatment.

Uses in woodworking

The construction industry now frames, sheathes, and floors with hemlock. Mills turn the wood into windows, frame-and-panel doors, moldings, and paneling. Due to its strength and wear resistance, hemlock also becomes reliable ladders and stair components.

Ease of machining and finishing have made hemlock an increasingly popular alternative to hardwood for furniture and cabinets. Lack of pitch and resin also makes hemlock ideal for a sauna's dry heat.

Cost and availability

Vast logging operations on the Pacific Northwest coast keep hemlock widely available in the West and Midwest. On the East Coast, even availability of local hemlock will be spotty.

If you need them, thick boards up to 14" wide aren't rare. And, hemlock costs less than Ponderosa or white pine.

HICKORY

Tougher than nails, and versatile, too

Because he fought tenaciously at the Battle of New Orleans in 1815, General Andrew Jackson's soldiers nicknamed him Old Hickory. His Tennesseans knew the wood well enough to make that comparison, since it grew abundantly in their state. If something had to be tough and strong, they made it of hickory—from ax, hammer, pick, and shovel handles to wagon spokes, hitch trees, and rims. Worked green, it became chairs.

The Choctaws and other Indians of the lower Mississippi River Valley had long used hickory for bows and baskets, but they also drew on its sap for sweet syrup and sugar and its nuts for cakes and meal. The pioneers who followed Davy Crockett valued hickory as firewood, too (it produces 24 million Btus per cord, about the same output as 200 gallons of No. 2 fuel oil). They also smoked ham and bacon with hickory.

Wood identification

North America claims 16 species of hickory, of which the most abundant and commercially important is the shagbark (*Carya ovata*). Other species native to the eastern half of the U.S. and Canada include the shellbark, bitternut, mockernut, pignut, water, swamp, and pecan. The hardwood lumber industry, though, doesn't distinguish between them.

Although hickory grows best in bottomland soils, you'll find it on loamy hillsides as well as rocky slopes. In the forest, hickory will grow to 140' tall and a diameter of 30", frequently with no branches for 50–60'.

Shagbark and shellbark hickory have long, loose plates of gray bark that appear to be peeling off the trunk. The bark of other hickories varies from furrowed to ridged, but always has a gray color. Hickories generally have from five to seven oblong, pointed leaflets per leaf stem, including a grouping of three at the tip. The fruit develops during the summer into woody four-lobed husks up to 2" long that contain the nut.

Generally straight-grained and coarse-textured, air-dried hickory

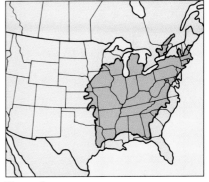

Natural range

weighs about 50 pounds per cubic foot. Hickory heartwood varies from tan to brownish-red. The sapwood is nearly white. Although some woods equal hickory in a single property, such as hardness or stiffness, not one commercially available wood can match it in the combination of hardness, bending strength, stiffness, and shock resistance.

Uses in woodworking

Traditionally, hickory has been used for objects that require strength and must take abuse—tool and implement handles, ladder rungs, and wagon wheels. In sports, hickory became hockey sticks, tennis rackets, bows, skis, and even fishing rods. Manmade materials have replaced hickory in
continued

HICKORY
continued

Hickory

many of these products today, but the wood still lends itself to chairs, rockers, stools, and tables—and any project requiring bent wood.

Availability

Hickory is plentiful throughout the eastern U.S., and its cost is low—about $2 per board foot. You'll find hickory plywood available, too, but if it's specifically pecan, it commands a premium price. Veneer costs 50 cents a square foot.

Remember that hardwood retailers may mix pecan boards in with other hickories and sell them all as hickory. Since pecan tends to have a more pinkish tone, it could alter staining and finishing results if mixed with tan-colored hickories in the same project. So for best results, sort if it's possible.

Machining methods

Because hickory's hardness even tops sugar maple, you'll definitely need carbide-tipped blades and cutters for your power tools. With that caution in mind, follow these additional tips:

• To avoid surface chipping when planing hickory, feed the wood at a slight angle.

• Feed hickory slowly when ripping, allowing the blade plenty of time to clear itself of sawdust. Crosscutting with a carbide blade poses no problems.

• Jointing straight-grained stock should be effortless, but occasional wavy-figured wood may chip, so take lighter cuts.

• In steam-bending hickory, use only the straightest-grained stock, then make arcs slightly tighter than needed. Pull the arch wider for an exact fit.

• Use only spurred bits and slower drill-press speeds when drilling hickory, and clear the bit often on thick stock to avoid burnishing.

• To avoid tearout, take light routing passes with a consistent feed rate.

• Avoid cross-grain sanding on hickory because it scratches. Where grains meet at right angles, do your cleanup with a cabinet scraper or random-orbit sander.

• For best results when gluing, use an adhesive with longer open time, such as white glue. Lay down a light coat, briefly join the pieces, then pull apart to allow glue to partially setup before reassembling them.

• Always drill pilot holes for fasteners in hickory, otherwise the wood may split.

• Although hickory responds to all stains and finishes equally well, you may want to fill the grain for ultimate smoothness.

Carving comments

Although hickory seldom finds its way into carvers' hands because of its extreme hardness, should you wish to tackle some of this tough wood, try these tactics:

• In addition to a shallow gouge bevel of 15°–20°, grind a bevel of 10° on the backside of the gouge tip, an always helpful trick for difficult hardwoods.

• Begin with medium cutting burn if you plan to power carve. The heavy bite of coarse cutters will chip the wood.

Turning tips

• Like most very hard woods, hickory poses no problems in between-centers turning, such as for chair parts, if you use sharp shearing tools (and resharpen them as they become dull).

• If you have to sand before applying a finish, avoid scratches by sanding with the lathe shut off, and only with the grain.

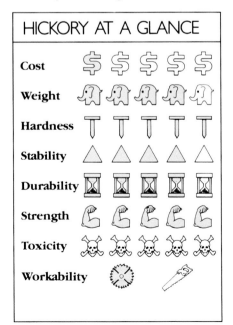

HICKORY AT A GLANCE				
Cost	$	$	$	$ $
Weight	🐘	🐘	🐘	🐘 🐘
Hardness	T	T	T	T T
Stability	△	△	△	△ △
Durability	⧖	⧖	⧖	⧖ ⧖
Strength	💪	💪	💪	💪 💪
Toxicity	☠	☠	☠	☠ ☠
Workability	🪚		🪚	

HOLLY

The snow-white wood of winter

Traditionally, decking the halls with boughs of holly marked the beginning of yuletide. The ancient Romans probably started this tradition—they used holly to decorate for *Saturnalia,* their celebration of the winter solstice. Today, the gathering of holly's thick, green, spiky leaves with bright red berries has become a seasonal industry along our southeastern seaboard.

Holly's connotation was not always joyful, however. Before there were laws to prevent such practices, purveyors of live songbirds as pets caught their pretty prey with the help of the holly tree. They mashed its bark to obtain a sticky, gluelike substance called birdlime, which was spread on tree branches. When the precious songsters alighted, they became stuck and were easily captured for market.

More favorably, holly leaves and berries have been touted in folklore as a cure for smallpox, a speedy

mender of broken bones, and an all-around lucky charm.

The wood has quite a reputation. As the whitest wood known, holly provides inlay for expensive furniture, the bodies of fine brushes, and even imitation ivory piano keys.

Wood identification

You can find 175 species of holly growing practically around the world, with the largest number in Brazil and Guiana. Thirteen species grow in the U.S. alone, but commercial loggers harvest only the largest of these, *Ilex opaca.*

In a range that extends south from Massachusetts to Florida and west to the Missouri River, holly varies in size from a bush to a tree of 50' or more in height. Northern winters keep holly small, but it thrives in Arkansas and east Texas. There, holly trees develop a dense, pyramidal shape with many short, horizontal branches. The broad, leatherlike leaves feature sharp prickles—nature's way of fending off animal browsers. By midwinter, red or yellow berries develop on female trees where blossoms once brightly flowered.

The bark of holly tends to be patternless, rough-textured, and medium gray, often with a tinge of olive. Older trees feature wartlike outgrowths. Weighing in at about 36 pounds per cubic foot dry, holly rates as moderately heavy and hard, but not strong. With indistinct, fine grain, the wood of holly displays no figure.

Color ranges from an almost pure white sapwood to heartwood with a creamy tone, and the two can be indistinguishable. To prevent a permanent discoloration called "blue stain," loggers cut holly only in the winter months, then process it quickly.

Working properties

Holly's hardness makes it difficult to work with hand tools. It does glue easily, however, and it resists splitting from screws and nails if you use pilot holes. Due to holly's extremely fine grain, it sands to ultimate smoothness.

Holly also accepts stain admirably—so much so that it was once called "dye wood."

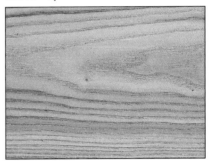

Holly heartwood

Uses in woodworking

You won't find many projects made entirely of holly, but it does make a striking accent when combined with darker woods. In marquetry, holly contributes its natural whiteness, or it can be colored as needed.

Because of its unusually tight grain, holly often becomes the choice of carvers and wood-block engravers. It also turns exceptionally well.

Cost and availability

Holly grows singly rather than in stands, and loggers harvest it along with other hardwoods. In the South, for example, where it reaches a large size, holly can be found mixed in and sold with soft maple, and you might have to find your holly by sorting through a soft maple pile. Otherwise, holly normally will be available from dealers specializing in hardwoods. You can buy holly veneers from marquetry supply houses. If you live far from its source, holly can cost as much as $5 per board foot.

HONDURAS MAHOGANY

The classic choice in tropical timber

The first mahogany to reach England was in the shape of ships—those of the Spanish Armada that later succumbed to the English fleet's cannonballs. That was in 1588, more than 30 years after the Spanish explorer Hernando Cortes discovered mahogany in the Caribbean.

Although English shipbuilders marveled at the new seagoing stock, it was the joiners who really appreciated this New World treasure. They could span greater lengths and widths than with any other wood available, due to the sheer size of the mahogany timbers.

By the late 1700s, the now-famous English cabinetmakers Chippendale, Hepplewhite, and Sheraton were shaping mahogany into classic furniture styles that kept the wood prominent for 150 years. Today's woodworker still finds delight in working mahogany into elegant cabinets, desks, tables, and other furniture.

Wood identification

Often referred to in the wood trade as Tropical American mahogany, Honduras mahogany (*Swietenia macrophylla*) grows throughout much of Central and South America, including southern Mexico. However, the first mahogany discovered by Spanish explorers was Cuban mahogany (*Swietenia mahagoni*), a species no longer commercially available. Another true mahogany exists in Africa—African mahogany (*Khaya ivorensis*). Philippine mahogany isn't a mahogany at all, but rather a *Shorea* species called lauan.

In the tropical forest, Honduras mahogany sometimes attains 150' heights and diameters of 72". Trees planted and grown for lumber on plantations (found in mahogany's natural range and the South Pacific), run smaller. Honduras mahogany on the stump has a

Natural range

heavily buttressed trunk base, scaly gray bark, and leaves displaying six to eight leaflets arranged on a single stem, much like those of the black walnut tree.

Honduras mahogany wood has straight, semi-open grain and a color that ranges from yellow-brown to dark red, depending on where it grows. With age, though, mahogany of all colors becomes a rich, dark red-brown. The wood also may display exceptional fiddleback, quilt, and ribbon-stripe figure.

A bit lighter than maple at 32 pounds per cubic foot, Honduras mahogany matches oak in strength. The wood also withstands moisture, resists fire and decay, and remains stable in use.

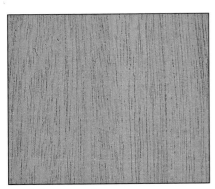

Straight-grained

Ribbon-striped

Uses in woodworking

Mahogany claims the qualities that make it the ideal stock for majestic desks, tables, and large cabinets. Both turners and carvers find the wood suited for intricately detailed work. And, today's boat-builders, like those centuries ago, turn to Honduras mahogany for structural members, decking, and trim.

Availability

Due to the tree's size, Honduras mahogany boards usually run wide and long. Expect to pay about $5 per board foot. Veneer offers the widest range of figure, but it will cost you $1 to $3 per square foot.

Machining methods

Paul McClure, *WOOD*® magazine's consultant on wood technology, calls Honduras mahogany "the wood by which all other woods are measured." By that, he means you couldn't ask for a better wood to work. And, all the craftsmen we asked agree with him. *So, note our advice, and enjoy this singular stock:*

• We don't know exactly why, but Honduras mahogany produces extremely fine dust during some machining operations. And, the dust hangs in the air longer than that of other woods. So, wear a respirator.

• Because of this mahogany's hardness and straight grain, it surfaces with minimal tearout. The wood even proves forgiving if you accidentally feed it into the jointer against the grain. Sharp knives leave nearly glass-smooth results free of mill marks. Feed figured stock into a planer slowly and at a slight angle. Otherwise, the wood grain may chip and tear on you.

• You can rip Honduras mahogany equally well with steel or carbide-tipped blades. However, blades with more than 28 teeth increase the chance of burning.

• Don't take chances on the wood splintering while cross-cutting. With a handsaw or power tools, always use a fence or backing board as a chip breaker on the exit side.

• Honduras mahogany cuts beautifully with a jigsaw or scrollsaw.

• Rout this wood with sharp bits (and don't forget the dust mask) for mark-free results. The grain "frizzes" with dull bits.

• You won't have problems joining Honduras mahogany, as all types of glue work well.

• Although the wood easily sands smooth, filling its open grain results in the sleekest surface.

• Choose any type of stain or finish for your Honduras mahogany project because the wood accepts them all equally. For outdoor projects, rely on a spar varnish or exterior polyurethane. It also takes and holds paint exceptionally well, but you'll need a primer coat and several top coats to completely fill the wood's open grain.

Carving comments

• Honduras mahogany became *the* wood for classic furniture because it was great to carve with knives and gouges and took detail. That holds true today. Power carvers should, however, adopt a light touch because motorized bits can get overly aggressive.

Turning tips

• To avoid chipping, round down Honduras mahogany with a ¾" gouge at 800–1,000 rpm.

• Turn off the lathe for final sanding, and sand with the grain.

• Don't apply finish to spinning wood because the open grain of Honduras mahogany momentarily collects the material. Then, as it spins, the finishing material flows from the grain to form what look like wrinkles.

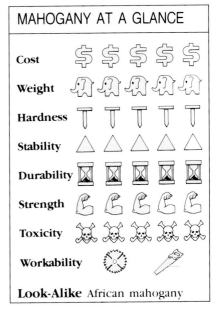

MAHOGANY AT A GLANCE	
Cost	💲 💲 💲 💲 💲
Weight	
Hardness	
Stability	
Durability	
Strength	
Toxicity	
Workability	
Look-Alike	African mahogany

KOA

Hawaii's hardwood soldier of the sea

Had the 18th-century explorer Captain James Cook been a woodworker with an eye for fine stock, he would have shaken his head in disbelief on his first Hawaiian landing. For in that Pacific paradise, natives had for centuries depended on huge outrigger canoes made from hollowed-out logs of a brightly hued hardwood. In them, they traveled hundreds of miles from island to island for war or trade. In fact, the early Hawaiians honored their canoe wood for its seaworthiness by naming it *koa-ka,* meaning "valiant soldier."

The English shortened the native word to koa. And, they no doubt quickly discovered that the beautiful wood had potential for more than dugout canoes.

By the late 1800s, items of koa appeared in U.S. ports, brought by returning missionaries. Attracted by the color and figure of the new wood, furniture makers, architects, and coachbuilders demanded logs. Nowhere, though, did anyone sing the gorgeous wood's praises louder than in Hawaii. There, craftsmen made koa ukuleles, an instrument introduced by Portuguese sailors.

Wood identification

Koa *(Acacia koa)* grows in quantity only in the Hawaiian islands. There, it grows everywhere—from the beaches to the volcanic peaks. Koa trees in Hawaii show no preference for a particular soil type or climate.

Mature koa trees reach 120' heights and 8' diameters. In stands, their trunks can be free of branches for 80'. Open-grown koa trees, however, nearly imitate live oak trees with numerous spreading branches that form wide, open crowns.

Koa's bark appears gray colored, flaky, and fissured. Branches display clusters of small, light-green, pointed leaves.

At about 50 pounds per cubic foot, air-dry, koa weighs about 25 percent more than black walnut. Koa, like walnut, has high crush resistance and shock absorbency. Unlike walnut, however, koa's grain interlocks, opening the door for exceptional fiddleback figure.

Koa's thin, light-colored sapwood surrounds a heartwood that some woodworkers describe as lustrous, swirled marble. Primarily reddish brown to dark brown, the wood occasionally carries colorful tones of gold, black, and deep purple.

Working properties

Due to koa's interlocking grain, you'll find that it has a greater bending strength and stiffness than walnut. It works quite easily with both hand and power tools, except that it may burn when routed or sawed cross-grain. So, keep cutting edges sharp and avoid a slow feed rate. Plane curly or fiddleback koa at a slight angle to avoid tearing the grain.

You'll have best success joining koa with screws as well as glue, since occasional resin pockets sometimes prevent solid adhesion with glue alone. These same resins, however, make the wood resistant

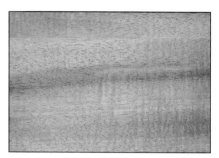

Fiddleback koa

Plain-sawed koa

to insects and fungus. And, you can sand koa to a silky finish.

Uses in woodworking

Koa ranks as a cabinet wood of exceptional beauty and quality. You can work it into fine furniture, sculpture, turnings, and musical instruments. Because of its shock resistance, it makes exceptional gunstocks. Due to its decay resistance, koa also performs well as boat trim. As veneer, especially with fiddleback figure, koa becomes costly architecture paneling.

Cost and availability

In the early seventies, koa was readily available in the mainland U.S. Then, it practically disappeared in the marketplace because Hawaii's main koa mill ceased operation. Now, through the efforts of smaller mills in the islands, you can buy the wood once again—at a premium price of about $7 per board foot. Plain-sliced, nonfigured veneer costs about $1.50 per foot—double for figured.

MAGNOLIA

The hardwood that sets bees buzzing

Referring to the tree's large and showy blooms, botanists call magnolia the most splendid tree in America's forests. Early settlers, though, were more impressed with practicality than beauty. In the southern reaches of the Allegheny Mountains, these hardy pioneers collected the conelike fruits that followed magnolia's flowers, then steeped and distilled them into a medicine said to ward off "autumnal fever."

In far more ancient times, the magnolia and its blooms actually played a major role in the evolution of hardwood trees. It seems that conifers, the dominant tree in primeval woodlands, relied on the whims of the wind for pollination and survival. The magnolia, however, developed the trait of producing fragrant flowers that attracted voracious beetles. Then, just as bees do now, the beetles traveled from tree to tree, reliably pollinating and propagating the species.

Today, southern magnolia and cucumber, its cousin, represent a significant slice of the southeastern hardwood lumber industry. Marketed as magnolia, both woods find their way into the hands of knowing craftsmen.

Wood identification

You'll find cucumber *(Magnolia acuminata)* in mixed hardwood stands from southern New York to Florida, and west through Illinois to Iowa and Texas. Southern magnolia *(Magnolia grandiflora)* prefers the warmer areas of the range. Other species of magnolia, cultivated as ornamentals due to their blooms, may grow as far north as Wisconsin, but not in commercial quantities.

In the forest, cucumber can measure 100' tall and 4' or more in diameter. Its brown, deeply furrowed bark resembles that of elm. In late May and June, the tree sports greenish-yellow flowers hiding amidst its leaves. Southern magnolia, with its scaly, light gray-green bark, averages only 80' tall and seldom attains 3' in diameter. Fragrant, creamy white flowers, often 10" across, decorate its branches from June through October.

Similar in weight to cherry, the wood of both magnolias is light yellowish-brown and plain-featured. Sometimes, it contains purple-colored mineral streaks that add interest.

Working properties

Magnolia has hard, fine-textured, straight-grained wood that some people might mistake for maple. And, like maple, magnolia works easily with power tools. It also won't warp when thin-sawed, turns well, and steam bends.

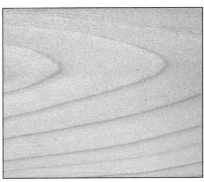

Magnolia heartwood

Because magnolia resists splitting and glues exceptionally well, you'll have no trouble joining it. You can plane the wood to a smooth surface that requires little sanding. Due to its fine grain, you won't have to fill before finishing with your choice of paint, stain, or clear coatings.

Uses in woodworking

Because magnolia remains stable after seasoning, it was once the standard wood for venetian-blind slats. That same stability makes it an acceptable substitute for yellow poplar. Cabinet carcasses and furniture, toys, and interior trim all fair well when made of this widely unappreciated wood. Use it for turned bowls and other food containers, too, since it doesn't impart a taste or carry an odor.

Cost and availability

Where it's sold, magnolia usually costs the same as yellow poplar, about $1.25 per board foot. In the South and Southeast, you'll find it more readily available, and in boards up to 2" thick. Four-inch square turning stock also is marketed. Due to lack of demand, magnolia isn't made into veneer.

MESQUITE

Dark mesquite

Light mesquite

Prime for steak, better for stock

Four decades following the fall of the Alamo, the people of San Antonio paved the streets leading to this Texas shrine with mesquite slabs. Today, street maintenance crews occasionally uncover remnants of the wood, still sound.

In the eyes of southwestern Indians, mesquite was shade and sustenance. They ate the tree's bean pods, turned its sap into gum, dye, medicine, and sewed with its thorns. The Indians relied on the wood for fuel and arrows.

Learning from the native Americans, pioneer hands worked mesquite into construction timbers, railroad ties, fence posts, wagon wheels, and sturdy tables and chairs.

Because most craftsmen only equate mesquite with the barbecue grill, a group called *Los Amigos del Mesquite* (Friends of Mesquite) promotes the wood as furniture-class stock. Due to their efforts, mesquite's reputation as quality cabinet wood seems to be spreading.

Wood identification

It's estimated that the three varieties of mesquite *(Prosopis glandulosa, juliflora, and pubescens)* cover some 75 million acres of Texas alone. These hardy trees also extend into Arizona, Oklahoma, and Mexico.

In desert areas, mesquite develops more as a shrub than a tree. More favorable conditions allow it to grow to about 50' tall with a single, though somewhat crooked, trunk up to 3' in diameter.

Mesquite, with its chocolate-colored, furrowed bark, isn't difficult to identify. Its wide, spreading canopy of frequently twisted branches sports long, thin leaves composed of evenly spaced leaflets. Bean pods up to 8" long follow the tree's bright, yellowish-white spring flowers. And, the short, sharp thorns amidst the leaves painfully pierce passing flesh.

Mesquite wood has fine, tightly interlocked grain. A narrow band of tan sapwood borders the deep brown heartwood.

Working properties

Mesquite remains quite stable during seasoning. Since the shrinkage occurs evenly, the wood sustains few drying defects. That's why carvers and turners work the wood green—it dries without checking.

Mesquite requires power tools because it's heavier than both oak and maple, but much harder. And, since it's rather brittle and contains a high percentage of silica, the wood demands sharp cutting edges.

Due to the wood's brittleness and silica content, you must join it with both adhesives and screws. And, adhesives work best when you wipe the surfaces with lacquer thinner.

Mesquite sands silky smooth with little effort. Like a true cabinet wood, it accepts oils and topcoats equally well.

Uses in woodworking

Craftsmen draw upon mesquite for furniture, carvings, and turnings. In the home, it serves as attractive, hard-wearing flooring and decorative items such as fireplace mantels. It also makes premium gunstocks and knife handles.

Cost and availability

Although mesquite has not attained commercial importance, many small enterprises throughout the Southwest sell the wood. You'll find it most frequently as turning squares and blocks, and as lumber in 1X8 and 2X8 sizes up to 5' long.

Prices range from $3 per board foot for nonselect wood to $10 or more for premium stock. Veneer isn't available.

For a list of mesquite suppliers and information concerning Los Amigos del Mesquite, write: *Ken E. Rogers, P.O. Box 310, Lufkin, TX 75901.*

NORTHERN RED OAK

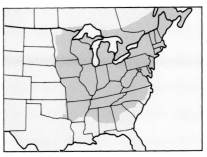

From men-of-war to kitchen cabinets, always number one

To England's ancient druids, the oak symbolized strength. Warlike Norsemen even cherished pieces of the wood as charms to protect them from evil. But to the Greeks, Romans, and later seafaring nations, oak meant sturdy men-of-war and reliable merchant ships. In fact, England and France reserved whole forests for use in building their fleets. That's why red oak from North America saw immediate popularity when it was introduced to those countries in the early 18th century. Within a few years, northern red oak substituted for native English and European oak species and was crafted into furniture and paneling.

Even after centuries of popularity, northern red oak still outsells all other hardwoods. And luckily, it's plentiful, comprising about one fifth of the standing timber species grouped as red oak.

Wood identification

The broad, spreading crown of the northern red oak (*Quercus rubra*) shades the landscape in a sweeping range that covers nearly half the U.S. and much of southeastern Canada, as shown on the map, *top right*. More commonly called red oak, but also known as eastern red oak, gray oak, and Canadian red oak, the tree can grow to 150' heights with trunks 6' in diameter in fertile upland forest soil. Open-grown trees more often approach only 70' with trunks that separate into several large branches.

Northern red oak has distinctive leaves up to 9" long, with a pointed bristle on each lobe tip. In the spring, flowing catkins of pollen-bearing flowers emerge amid the greenery. Acorns about 1" long develop every two years.

Rare is the board of northern red oak that carries a trace of its light-colored sapwood. Instead, the vast majority of northern red oak treats woodworkers to nicely figured heartwood with a pinkish tint.

You'll find that northern red oak has coarse-textured, straight, open grain. This hard, stiff, strong wood weighs 44 pounds per cubic foot dry—just a little more than walnut.

Natural range

Uses in woodworking

Ever since the early 1970s, northern red oak has been highly favored for kitchen cabinets, and still leads in appeal for all kinds of furniture as well as millwork and flooring. Turners and carvers, too, find the wood a choice stock for decorative projects.

Availability

Hardwood dealers and home centers offer northern red oak as lumber, veneer, plywood, turning squares, and dowels. But, all northern red oak won't be the same. Trees from the North—from the Appalachians on into Canada—grow slower and therefore have a more uniform color and a finer, easier-working texture than those from the South. Other characteristics remain the same, though. And, no matter where the wood hails from, board-foot price hovers around $3.

continued

NORTHERN RED OAK
continued

Machining methods

As most woodworkers will attest, red oak works wonderfully, but it does require power tools. Even then, the wood sometimes takes special handling. *Our observations:*

• Feed red oak on the jointer so that the knives' rotation follows the direction of the grain flow (see sketch, *below)*. Failure to do this generally produces chipping.

• Due to red oak's open, straight grain, it offers only moderate resistance to ripping.

• Red oak quickly dulls anything other than a carbide blade.

• Too fast a feed rate on the table or radial-arm saw, or with the router, can cause burning, although burns sand off easily.

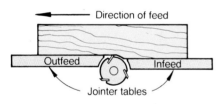

• Red oak tends to splinter. So, use shallow router passes on end grain and a backing board clamped to the exit side on cross-grain work.

• Metal, such as a clamp bar, touching glue squeeze-out produces a dark blue stain. Lay wax paper over the glue line.

• Red oak grips screws, but even with pilot holes, lubricating the threads with paraffin eases driving.

• Although red oak sands readily, try garnet paper for hand-sanding and with orbital sanders. For belt sanders, we prefer oxide-type abrasives. Swirls and other sanding marks come off nearly effortlessly.

• For the smoothest possible finish, fill red oak's grain with a paste-type filler. The filled wood (see photo *above, near right)* has less dramatic grain contrast, but it

Filled red oak

requires fewer coats to build the final finish. For a lighter fill, sand surfaces with Danish oil as a lubricant. The sanded-off fiber packs the grain.

Carving comments

Only the most accomplished carvers tackle hard red oak, and then mostly for relief work. You won't get far without a mallet and very sharp gouges. Some tips:

• Change from a shallow bevel (of 15°–20°) to a deeper bevel of 25°–30° when you rough-in the outline of a relief design. Your

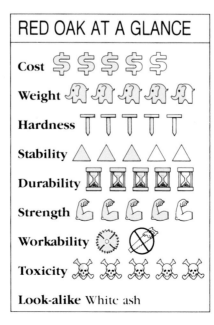

RED OAK AT A GLANCE

Cost	💲💲💲💲💲
Weight	🐘🐘🐘🐘🐘
Hardness	T T T T T
Stability	△ △ △ △ △
Durability	⧗ ⧗ ⧗ ⧗ ⧗
Strength	💪💪💪💪💪
Workability	⚙ ⊘
Toxicity	☠ ☠ ☠ ☠ ☠
Look-alike	White ash

Unfilled red oak

gouges stay sharp longer. Then, when it's time to do the details and complete the carving, grind to a shallow bevel again for shaving.

• *Our advice:* Avoid slices along straight grain with stop cuts.

Turning tricks

• When turning between centers, combat splinters by entering the wood with a sharp tool, such as a clean-cutting skew, and taking shallow cuts, especially when first rounding the turning square.

• *Our turning tip:* Keep tools sharp to cut rather than abrade. And, don't start at one end and cut all the way to the other. Remove wood a little at a time in each section because the grain may run on a bias and splinter away.

PECAN

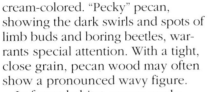

The "great spirit" hickory

Algonquin Indians of the southern Mississippi River basin region believed the pecan tree embodied the Great Spirit—perhaps because this one species provided so many of life's essentials. Pecan, a member of the hickory family, furnished nuts for eating, oil for cooking, and wood for implements and fuel. Pioneers, introduced to its bounty by the Indians, named this tree in honor of the Algonquin chief Peccan.

A North American native, pecan has been traced to the Cretaceous period of 130 million years ago. Fossils found in Oregon and Washington prove that pecan was growing while dinosaurs roamed in what was then a much-warmer climate.

Once cherished for dining and living room furniture, pecan is now valued far more for its annual nut crop than its wood.

Wood identification

Belonging to the genus *Carya,* which accounts for approximately 22 hickory species throughout North America, pecan is often cut, graded, and marketed simply as hickory.

Pecan *(Carya illinoensis)*, however, has a warmer, pink-tinted tone than does hickory. Its heartwood ranges from light to medium-tan in color and the sapwood tends to be cream-colored. "Pecky" pecan, showing the dark swirls and spots of limb buds and boring beetles, warrants special attention. With a tight, close grain, pecan wood may often show a pronounced wavy figure.

In forest habitat, pecan rarely reaches 100' in height. Growing in the open, or in orchards, pecan trees may achieve 160' but will have shorter, divided trunks with many upreaching branches (the better to bear nuts).

Pecan grows primarily from southern Indiana southwestward into Texas. However, it has been successfully introduced into other mild-climate areas (Florida and Georgia, for instance) for its nut crop.

Working properties

If you've used hard maple successfully, you'll have no problem working pecan. The wood has remarkable strength, hardness, elasticity, and shock resistance—qualities some woods claim individually but that combine only in pecan. Because pecan possesses this all-around toughness, it can't easily be worked with hand tools—carbide-tipped cutters on power tools become a necessity.

While pecan shrinks considerably during drying, it remains fairly stable once seasoned. When dry, pecan weighs 42–52 pounds per cubic foot.

Pecan bends with little effort and glues well, but its tendency to split necessitates pilot holes for screws

Pecan lumber

Pecan-veneered plywood

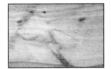

Pecky pecan

and nails. The hardness of pecan translates into a wood that can be brought to a mirrorlike finish.

Uses in woodworking

While 80 percent of all hickory goes for tool handles and rugged farm implement parts, pecan wood becomes quality office desks and chairs. It also finds its way into home wall paneling and commercial architectural veneers. For long-wearing chair parts—legs, backs, and rungs—pecan may be unequaled.

Cost and availability

Some large hardwood suppliers label pecan specifically. When it's mixed with hickory, you have to sort to find the pecan.

Pecan is available in boards up to 8" wide and 8' long. Pecan veneers are widely offered, too, but pecan-faced plywood may be harder to find.

You can buy pecan fairly inexpensively. A board foot of pecan can be purchased for about half the cost of the same amount of red oak, for instance, a fact that reflects pecan's diminished popularity as a furniture wood.

PONDEROSA PINE

The West's tall, lean, and rugged softwood

Exploring the headwaters of the Missouri River in 1804, the Lewis and Clark expedition sighted towering stands of trees more majestic than any they'd known before. Twenty years later, the English botanist David Douglas discovered these same trees growing along the Spokane River in what is now Washington state. Because of their ponderous dimensions and the comparative heaviness of their wood for pine, he named them "Ponderosa."

Ponderosa pine, Montana's state tree, is truly the wood of the West. Indians wove its long needles into baskets and jewelry. Ranchers felled it for barns and bunkhouses. On July 4, 1876, Arizona lumberjacks stripped branches from the tallest ponderosa they could find, and hoisted the American flag in celebration of the nation's centennial—that's how the town of Flagstaff got its name.

One of the most commercially important trees in the United States, ponderosa pine also has the distinction of being the subject of a Supreme Court ruling. A 1934 decision protects it from being sold under any name except ponderosa.

Wood identification

Occasionally referred to as Western yellow pine and black-jack pine, ponderosa pine *(Pinus ponderosa)* is one of 35 pines native to North America. Mature trees have cinnamon to orange-brown, scaly bark on a trunk up to 8' in diameter at chest height.

Needles up to 10" long grow in threes along its branches, which also bear 6"-long, brown cones. "Young" ponderosa pines (under 100 years old) display dark brown to nearly black bark; hence the nickname blackjack pine.

In its native mountain slopes and well-drained uplands, the ponderosa can reach 200' high. It is also a long-lived pine; specimens 500 years old are not uncommon.

Ponderosa pine stands tall in the saddle among softwoods. It is yellowish-white, hard, fine grained, and strong, yet light. Dry, it weighs about 25 pounds per cubic foot.

Growing in 11 western states, as well as in the Black Hills of South Dakota, ponderosa pine has the greatest range of any commercial tree in America—approximately one third of the U.S.

Ponderosa with heartwood

Ponderosa sapwood

Working properties

As the finest of the pines available in volume today, this wood has all the excellent working qualities you could ask for: You can cut and shape it by hand as well as with power tools; it glues extremely well; and it doesn't split readily.

Because of ponderosa's texture, uniform cell structure, and comparative hardness for a softwood, it stains and finishes exceptionally well.

Uses in woodworking

The volume of ponderosa harvested makes it a mainstay of the construction industry. Knotty pine paneling and furniture for the popular country look come from this tree.

In the workshop, ponderosa pine easily fashions into furniture, wood novelties, toys, pastry boards, and cabinets. Carvers often choose it over other woods.

Cost and availability

Ponderosa pine is available in both "construction" dimension and hardwood dimension, such as 6/4. This makes for complex grading standards. Common grade lumber goes from No. 1 down to No. 5. Select grades, for furniture and cabinets, consist of B and Better (the highest), C-Select, D-Select, and Factory Select. The lowest grades are No. 1, No. 2, and No. 3 Shop.

Cost, of course, varies with the grade, but even top grades carry more moderate prices than some cabinet-class hardwoods.

RED ALDER

The West Coast's weed tree goes to market

There's a transformation going on in the Northwest logging country. A tree long considered an ugly duckling is finally becoming a swan!

Red alder, the Pacific coast's most abundant hardwood, has been around for at least 40 million years—often in too-great numbers. Timber producers even called it a weed because this fast-grower pops up in burned or logged out forest areas, sometimes menacing the growth of commercially important softwood seedlings.

Over time, though, foresters began to realize something special about red alder. It resists a wildfire's consuming flames. Taking advantage of this, they planted red alder along logging roads for fire breaks to protect stands of conifers. Today, after loggers harvest the stands, they turn to the red alder for logs to supply a steadily developing market demand.

Red alder has gained respect as an absorbent pulp for paper towels, and as a tough pallet material. Even in woodworkers' eyes, red alder has emerged as an attractive, low-cost, easily worked, and durable stock.

Wood identification

All along its coastal range from Alaska to California, red alder (*Almus rubra*) seldom grows alone. It typically occurs in groves along streams, rivers, and on slopes, where soil is moist and fertile. In perfect conditions, such as around Washington's Puget Sound, red alders reach a peak height of 130' and 36" maximum diameter.

You could easily mistake red alder for aspen or birch because of its smooth, very light gray bark with mottled markings often spotted by moss. The leaves appear similar, too, except red alder's are nearly twice as long and coated with short hairs on the underside. In the fall, the still-green leaves swirl to the ground.

Red alder's yellowish-white heartwood quickly turns a reddish color when exposed to air. However, the brightness fades to a flesh shade during seasoning. The wood's straight, close grain has subtle figure.

Working properties

At 28 pounds per cubic foot, dry red alder weighs about two-thirds less than red oak. A little harder than butternut and not quite as strong as mahogany, the wood works easily even with hand tools. It accepts nails and screws readily, and holds them well. The wood has a good reputation for gluing.

We recommend a sealer or shellac wash coat before staining to avoid blotchiness. While red alder's grain may raise if you use a water-based stain, the wood sands easily to a smooth finish. All kinds of clear top coats adhere readily.

Uses in woodworking

Due to red alder's stability and good gluing properties, manufacturers often use it as plywood core stock. Because it requires little cleanup sanding, the wood has also become a favorite for factory-made, mass produced turnings. You'll find this wood being used on the West Coast for paneling, doors, millwork, unfinished furniture, and even water-bed frames.

Red Alder

At home, you can use red alder for practically any project calling for hardwood. It turns and carves easily, and is hard and strong enough for furniture and casework. Use it as a substitute for cherry, mahogany, and/or walnut.

Cost and availability

Now that red alder has become appreciated as woodworking stock, and is light to ship, its availability has spread from the West Coast to the Midwest. Competition from woods such as poplar and willow make red alder less likely to be found in the East.

Red alder comes in five grades. Selects and better, the finest grade, costs about $2 per board foot. And, you can often find red alder boards up to 3" thick.

REDWOOD

The forest's elder statesman

The giant of all nature's plants, the coastal redwood of California and Oregon can tower to the height of a 30-story building. Inland, the sierra redwood—though not as tall as its cousin—grows to immense circumference. In California's King's Canyon National Park, for instance, the General Ulysses S. Grant redwood contains enough wood to build 60 five-room houses! That Sierra redwood ranks as the world's second oldest living thing. Only an ancient bristlecone pine in the mountains above California's Death Valley surpasses its 32 centuries. Even the coastal species can survive 2,200 years.

Regardless of the Sierra redwood's massive size, it's the coastal redwood that lumbermen have harvested since 1777. That's when Indian workmen felled redwood trees in the hills around San Jose to provide the wood for the Spanish mission at Santa Clara.

Wood identification

As its name implies, the commercially important coastal redwood *(Sequoia sempervirens)* grows in a narrow, coastal range from southern Oregon to California's Monterey Bay. This mountainous habitat feeds necessary moisture through frequent rains and fog.

Coastal redwoods, with their thick, cinnamon-colored bark and small, flat green needles, grow from tiny seeds. In prime conditions, this fastest-growing conifer produces as much as 400 cubic feet (about 78,000 board feet) of growth per acre annually.

Natural range

Redwood has a warm, brownish-red color when sawed from the heart of the tree. Boards with sapwood have contrasting, cream-colored accents. Left unfinished to weather, all redwood turns gray.

Redwood lumber has either flat-grain feature (appearing wavy) or vertical (appearing straight), depending on how it was sawed. Beautifully figured burls produce costly veneer.

Redwood grading contains as many as 45 designations at the mill, but you need only concern yourself with these quality grades:

• *Clear all-heart* contains all heartwood with only minor surface defects on one side.

• *Clear,* the same quality as above, but with sapwood.

• *B-grade,* mixes heart and sapwood, with knots.

Clear all-heart vertical grain

Clear flat-grain with sapwood

Uses in woodworking

Natural chemicals in the heart-wood provide redwood with outstanding durability. It resists water, insects, and decay-causing fungi, making it ideal for any outdoor project. Redwood also makes excellent millwork and siding. Because the wood imparts no odor or taste to liquids, it's prime stock for water tanks and other vessels.

Availability

Redwood costs more the farther you live from the tree's home range. In California, for instance, clear all-heart runs much less per board foot for 1x6" stock, as compared to the price in New York. Unlike hardwoods, redwood lumber comes in nominal sizes—1x6, 1x8, 2x4, 4x4, and so on.

The availability of redwood in several grades often confuses buyers at the lumberyard. Follow these guidelines when buying for your woodworking projects:

• Construction on or near soil requires redwood grades featuring durable heartwood. Above-ground redwood projects can contain boards with sapwood.

• Architectural grades (Clear all-heart, Clear, and B Grade), sold kiln-dried, provide the finest material for attractive paneling, cabinetry and other interior or exterior project applications.

• Garden grades (Construction heart, Construction common, Merchantable heart, and Merchant-able) are usually air-dried, and have tight knots and other defects that only affect appearance. These grades are suitable for decks, porches, fences, gazebos, furniture, and other outdoor, garden-type projects.

Machining methods

Redwood, although considerably light at 23 pounds per cubic foot, has surprising structural strength. And, it remains stable when kiln-dried. However, the straight-grained wood does have a tendency to split and splinter, so take the following precautions:

• Planing requires a shallow cut to avoid chipping and tearout. Joint with a table-height setting that removes no more than 1/16" per pass.

• Ripping redwood poses no special problems, but crosscutting requires a fine-toothed blade to reduce splintering and tearout.

• Avoid tearout in cross-grain routing by using a backing board.

• Redwood joins easily with all types of glues. You will, however, want to drill pilot holes for screws and blunt nails to avoid splitting. And, because the soft wood can tear out in projects subject to stress, such as outdoor furniture, consider adding strength by joining with nuts and bolts.

• You'll find that all types of interior finishes are compatible with redwood. For exterior use, though, avoid clear varnishes and polyurethanes without ultraviolet-light (UV) inhibitors because organic compounds in the wood react with sunlight to break down these finishes rather quickly. Some penetrating finishes—formulated especially for redwood—retard the wood's tendency to turn gray. Other formulations renew the wood's natural color.

Carving comments

• Due to its softness and straight grain, redwood carves effortlessly. Beware of the wood's tendency to splinter, though.

• Redwood will take detail, but it lends itself best to outdoor signs and sculptural forms.

Turning tips

• Keep in mind that sharp tools reduce splinters and tearout.

• Reduce possible tearout in the end grain that appears in the bottom of bowls by sanding the vessel to final shape.

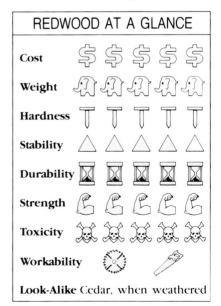

REDWOOD AT A GLANCE					
Cost	$	$	$	$	$
Weight					
Hardness					
Stability					
Durability					
Strength					
Toxicity					
Workability					
Look-Alike	Cedar, when weathered				

SASSAFRAS

The look-alike wood better known as tea

Native Americans turned the bounty of the land into the essentials of life. The tree that the Narragansett Indians called *sasauaka-pamuch* was no exception. Long before European explorers landed on the continent, the tree yielded its roots, bark, and leaves for a medicinal brew believed to cure everything from sore eyes to diarrhea.

Colonists coined the word *sassafras* from the Indian's language. And from the tree's healing properties, they coined profits from export. Sassafras tea was touted across the ocean as a tonic to "thin the blood and purify the system."

To those pioneers who used the wood, sassafras became well known as long lasting. Because it resists rot in contact with the ground, farmers sunk it for fence posts and split it for rails. Since it was light and absorbed little water, sassafras also was ideally suited for canoes and cooperage.

In the woodshop, sassafras often becomes a substitute for chestnut. It also resembles ash, and mixes well with it in furniture manufacturing.

Wood identification

Ancestors of sassafras *(Sassafras albidum),* a truly American species, grew across the continent during early geologic periods. Now, it's found from southern Maine south to central Florida and west to the Mississippi River Valley and eastern Texas.

In its northern range, sassafras rarely grows larger than shrub-size. But in favorable conditions in North Carolina and Tennessee, sassafras trees may reach 5' in diameter, 100' tall, and live 1,000 years.

Sassafras rarely grows in stands. Instead, it mixes with white oak, persimmon, and sweet gum. You can pick it out by its normally flat-topped crown or twisted branches sticking straight out from the trunk. Old trees have deeply furrowed, reddish-brown bark with flattened ridges, and appear as if they had been washed with light gray. The bark of young trees looks reddish, but has cracks instead of furrows.

Sassafras leaves are a dead giveaway—they have three long lobes, often mis-shapen, and varying in size, even on the same branch. If you have any doubt, sniff. All parts of the tree have a pleasant, medicinal odor.

Although its coarse grain mimics ash or chestnut, sassafras wood weighs less. Dry, it weighs only about 30 pounds per cubic foot. Wood from older trees has a red-brown color; from younger ones, a

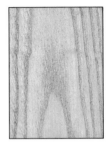

yellow-tan. There's little color difference between heartwood and sapwood.

Working properties

A soft hardwood, sassafras works easily with only hand tools. Planing, however, requires care so you don't lift the grain. And, you'll find the wood brittle and not very strong, characteristics that demand glue when joining. Fasteners alone won't hold in the wood.

Sanding sassafras poses no problem. It takes a fine finish.

Sassafras

Uses in woodworking

When not required to bear weight, sassafras blends undetectably with ash in furniture and cabinetry. And due to its likeness to chestnut, the wood often imitates the long-lost classic in antique reproductions. Woodturners and carvers with sharp tools easily work sassafras's unusual grain patterns into eye-catching pieces.

Cost and availability

The occasional sassafras sold by hardwood lumber outlets costs about $2 per board foot. It rarely will be more than 1" thick and wider than 8". When mixed and sold with ash, it carries a higher price. To be sure what you're buying, scrape or abrade a fresh surface to release the unmistakable odor of sassafras in the wood. Very seldom will you find sassafras sold as plywood or veneer.

SITKA SPRUCE

The softwood strong enough to fly

In the days when Russia claimed Baranof Island, off the coast of present-day Alaska, stands of spruce trees towered over it like 300'-tall sentinels. Botanist August Bongard was so impressed by these trees when he traveled there in the early 1800s that he named them Sitka, after the island's Russian capital.

Sitka spruce, so hardy that it grows farther north than any other conifer, also rates as the "strong-man" of softwoods. Indians long ago used its tough root tendrils to sew together their bark canoes.

In modern times, Sitka spruce, with reputedly the greatest strength-to-weight ratio of any wood, took to the air. The famous *Spruce Goose* amphibious airplane, built by millionaire entrepreneur Howard Hughes in the '40s, was made from this wood. So were the frames of some English WW II fighter planes. In air battles they were so small and fast they earned the name "mosquitoes."

Boatbuilders have always found Sitka spruce well suited for masts and oars, and luthiers love it for the soundboards of stringed instruments. However, much of this wood becomes millwork, or is made up into furniture, boxes, and crates. Even larger quantities end up as paper pulp because of the wood's long fibers.

Wood identification

Often called coast spruce and yellow spruce, Sitka spruce (*Picea sitchensis*) stands taller than any of the 18 spruce species found in the Northern Hemisphere. It grows in a coastal area about 50 miles wide and stretching some 2,000 miles from northern California to Kodiak Island, Alaska. It prefers low, wet valleys where the trees grow in dense stands and have no branches for the first 40' or more.

You'll be able to identify Sitka spruce by its size, the scaly, deep reddish-brown or purple bark, and its needles. Unique for a spruce, the needles of Sitka spruce grow flat, sharply pointed, and a bright bluish green. Flexible cones up to 4" long deve-lop over the sum-mer, finally opening to drop their seeds in the fall. Where the seeds land on moist ground, they readily germinate and grow.

The color of Sitka spruce wood ranges from nearly white to pink to light brown, and sometimes has a candy-stripe look. Heartwood tends to run slightly darker.

Working properties

Very straight-grained, Sitka spruce has less conspicuous growth rings than pine. It's also about 10 percent lighter, weighing 25 pounds per cubic foot air-dry.

In the shop, you'll find that it works easily with both hand and power tools. It nails, screws, and glues well, and takes a lustrous finish. However, because Sitka spruce is tough and stringy, band-sawing requires sharp, wide blades.

Uses in woodworking

Sitka spruce imparts no taste and gives off no odor, so use it for food canisters, boxes, and butter molds. Its strength and lightness make it perfect for painted furniture and shelving, as well as moldings and doors.

Quarter-sawn so the grain runs vertically, this wood becomes a top choice for the soundboards of guitars, dulcimers, and other stringed instruments. It flexes to aid sound.

Sitka spruce heartwood and sapwood

Sitka spruce heartwood

Cost and availability

On the West Coast and in the western states, you can buy Sitka spruce at lumberyards. Elsewhere, you have to special-order it, even in thin-cut soundboard stock from specialty suppliers. A top-grade soundboard will cost from $35 to $50. But price of construction-grade Sitka spruce approaches that of pine. Specially sawn, vertical grain lumber may cost $3 a board foot.

SUGAR MAPLE

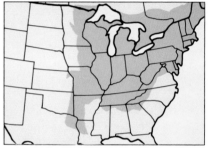

Hard as a rock, but how sweet it is!

Acer, part of the maple family's Latin, scientific name, means hard or sharp. And to the Romans, the wood was just that. From it, they made lance and pike shafts for battle. It was furniture, though, that bestowed the term "rock hard" on this traditional stock.

As the story goes, a colonial American cabinetmaker by the name of Rock promoted his work as "Rock's Hard Maple Furniture." That's why to this day many people refer to sugar maple as rock or rock-hard maple.

Sugar maple, although tough as its reputation, has a sweeter side. The other half of its genus name—*saccharum*—refers to its sap, a source of syrup and sugar.

Natural range

crown of many branches. All sugar maples when young have a smooth silvery bark that with age turns ash-gray and breaks into unevenly layered flakes or scales.

Sugar maple has palm-sized leaves with five pointed lobes that in the fall call forth brilliant shades of red and orange. In early summer, double-winged keys— the tree's inedible fruit—emerge.

Straight-grained, fine-textured, hard, strong, and at 44 pounds per cubic foot as heavy as red oak, the wood of sugar maple has high commercial value. Its sapwood, frequently 3–5" thick, appears much lighter in color than the slightly pinkish-tan heartwood. Both are sold.

Some trees produce spectacularly figured wood in curly, fiddleback, quilt, and bird's-eye.

Uses in woodworking

Known for its toughness and durability, sugar maple takes a pounding as bowling-lane surfaces, bowling pins, school desks, tool handles, and ladder rungs. On a gentler side, it's sugar maple that becomes much of the furniture we call "Early American." The wood

also shows up as cabinets, countertops, cutting boards, butcher block, and flooring.

Turners find figured sugar maple, particularly burls and intricately colored spalted stock, appealing for bowls. Fiddleback sugar maple has always been popular for the backs of stringed instruments, such as violins.

Availability

Sugar maple, sold all across the continent, often comes in board lengths of 12' and widths to 10". Large dealers may also offer figured wood as well as plain lumber. And, furniture squares, hardwood plywood, and figured veneers are easily obtained.

In abundant supply, sugar maple lumber sells for about $1.50 per board foot (slightly more for figured stock). Veneer, from plain to exquisitely figured, costs from 50 cents to $1 per square foot.

Practically all states east of the Great Plains boast sugar maple *(Acer saccharum),* which in a forest setting grows 70–130' tall with a diameter of 2–3'. Open-grown trees have shorter trunks with a rounded

Straight-grained sugar maple

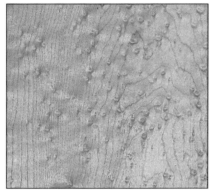
Bird's-eye sugar maple

Machining methods

Sugar maple isn't dubbed "hard maple" without reason. It dulls cutting edges, yet it chips. And, sugar maple burns more easily from cutting and machining than any other wood. *Here's how to overcome this wood's pesky traits:*

• Feed densely figured wood, such as bird's-eye, very slowly into the planer, and never plane it exactly to thickness. Leave some for sanding. Otherwise, the grain tears out in pocks. For hand-planing, set the iron at a 15°–20° angle.

• Dense, close-grained sugar maple demands a rip-profile blade with *no more than 28 teeth*. Sawdust won't accumulate, causing friction that heats the blade to burn the wood. If tearout occurs, allow for a ½" jointing pass to clean the edge.

• Crosscut figured wood with help from a backing board.

• Drill sugar maple at about 250 rpm, and back the bit out to clear chips. A stubby, spurred brad-point bit won't burn the wood as easily as one with long spurs. Burning glazes the wood.

• Avoid burning by routing only with bits that have ballbearing pilots. With speed control, rout slowly. Use a consistent feed rate.

• Lubricate screws.

• Sugar maple doesn't absorb glue immediately, sometimes

resulting in joint slippage from excess glue. If this happens, switch to a glue with longer open time (such as a white glue) and put down a lighter coat. Briefly join the pieces, then pull them apart and let the glue set up before reassembling.

Note: *Solid joinery usually requires a machined joint.*

• Don't oversand sugar maple with extremely fine paper, such as 400- or 600-grit. Excessive sanding burnishes the wood so that it won't readily accept stain. Avoid cross-grain sanding. Better yet, use a cabinet scraper.

• For even staining on sugar maple, first apply a wood conditioner, or use aniline dyes. Tinting the topcoat works, too.

Carving comments

• Sugar maple discourages the most accomplished carvers, but it does take very fine detail. *Here's how to handle it:*

• Even a shallow gouge bevel of 15°–20° erodes fast in this wood. To add edge longevity, grind a slight (10°) bevel on the *backside* of the gouge tip.

• Power carvers should start with medium-cut burrs, then follow with finer ones. Coarse-cutting burrs chip the wood.

Turning tips

• Sugar maple turns like a dream, even for beginners, and requires little or no sanding when sheared with sharp tools. *Here's two tips to avoid burning:*

• Don't let the turning tool's bevel ride in one spot very long.

• When sanding on the lathe, watch for abrasives wearing off. Bare sandpaper running against the wood will burn it, too.

SUGAR MAPLE AT A GLANCE					
Cost	💲	💲	💲	💲	💲
Weight	🐘	🐘	🐘	🐘	🐘
Hardness	T	T	T	T	T
Stability	△	△	△	△	△
Durability	⌛	⌛	⌛	⌛	⌛
Strength	💪	💪	💪	💪	💪
Toxicity	☠	☠	☠	☠	☠
Workability	🪚		🚫		
Look-Alike Yellow birch					

SWEET GUM

Sweet gum heartwood

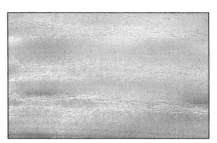

Sweet gum sapwood

The stock that stepped in when walnut went to war

Until the 1920s, few woodworkers had ever even seen a sweet gum board. Although sweet gum trees grew from Texas to Connecticut, little of the wood became lumber because of uncontrollable warping problems during seasoning.

When lumbermen finally discovered that sweet gum boards had to be either heartwood or sapwood—never containing both—for satisfactory drying, production boomed. By the 1930s, sweet gum climbed from commercial obscurity to a rank of seventh in hardwood usage.

Then, with the advent of World War II, most of the commercial walnut supply went to war as gunstocks. Only the wealthy could afford furniture made from the scant walnut remaining. So sweet gum stepped in as "poor man's walnut." Stained, the figured wood made a superb walnut imitation in economically priced furniture and radio cabinets. Sweet gum was even introduced to Europe as "satin walnut," and many board feet still sail in annual export.

In contrast to the come-from-behind popularity of sweet gum wood, sweet gum sap has always boasted a reputation. It has a delicate fragrance that at one time was extracted for scenting ladies' gloves. The sap also acts as an antiseptic for surface wounds, and a modern extraction, liquid storax, becomes an ingredient of styrene plastic.

Wood identification

Frequently called red gum because of its brightly colored fall foliage, sweet gum *(Liquidambar styraciflua)* tints autumn from southern Connecticut to Florida and as far west as Texas, Oklahoma, and southeast Missouri. In rich, moist soil, the tree grows to heights of 120' and diameters of 36".

The dark-gray, deeply furrowed bark on the main trunk of sweet gum trees often measures 1" thick. Limbs tend to have broken-patterned, wartlike bark resembling alligator skin.

Often heavily figured by streaks of darker shades, sweet gum's reddish-brown heartwood has a satiny appearance. Sapwood, marketed separately, ranges from a light pink to a pearl white, and seldom contains figure.

Working properties

Weighing slightly less than walnut, sweet gum heartwood has an interlocking, close grain and rates nearly as hard, stiff, and strong as walnut. Sapwood, however, doesn't come comparably close on these points.

The wood's grain demands that you use sharp hand or power tools to reduce tearing the fibers. Keeping that in mind, you'll find sweet gum—especially the sapwood—excellent for turning. And all sweet gum holds nails and screws well without splitting. However, before gluing heartwood, you should always wipe surfaces with alcohol.

Sweet gum takes stain evenly, and you can bring any finish to a beautiful luster with little effort. In fact, sweet gum heartwood's naturally attractive grain makes it look like an expensive cabinet wood.

Uses in woodworking

Use sweet gum sapwood for turned objects, treenware, and the hidden parts of furniture. You can work heartwood into furniture, cabinets, and interior trim. The wood's fragrance makes it a pleasant choice for the sides and bottoms of lingerie and linen drawers.

Cost and availability

Except for 3x3" turning stock, you'll rarely find sweet gum sapwood sold in the western states. Shipping costs prove prohibitive for this inexpensive wood. Heartwood, in both lumber and veneer, sells at retail throughout the U.S.

Board-foot prices for heartwood range between $2 and $3, compared to walnut at about $4. Veneer costs about $1 per foot. Sapwood, available only in lumber, costs less.

The highly figured heartwood of sweet gum becomes plywood and architectural panels. These products command top-dollar prices.

SYCAMORE

Ghost of the bottomlands

Fur trappers and traders plying Mississippi River tributaries in the 1700s didn't look far for canoe stock. The massive, bone-white trunks of the native sycamore—the preferred material for their huge dugout vessels—stood out like ghosts from other trees lining the waterways. And often, nature had already performed much of the work, partially hollowing the trunks by decay.

The sycamore easily met the size requirements for trade canoes that frequently measured 65' long. That's because among hardwoods, the sycamore is the hands-down winner for immense proportions. The largest known example in the United States shades a yard in Jeromesville, Ohio. It stands 129' tall, measures 15½' in diameter, and has a 105' crown spread.

In addition to sycamore's early use for canoes, the wood offered sound stock for cooperage and crates, tobacco and cigar boxes, butcher blocks, and saddletrees.

And luthiers found quarter-sawed sycamore perfect for the backs and sides of fiddles and other musical instruments.

Wood identification

The most widespread of three native sycamore species, the American sycamore *(Platanus occidentalis)* appears in rich, moist bottomland soils from Kansas to the Atlantic Ocean. Variously called planetree, buttonwood, and buttonball-tree, sycamore seldom grows in stands, but intermingles with other lowland hardwood trees.

In the best of conditions, sycamore attains 100' heights and diameters upwards of 10'. The area umbrellaed by the tree's spreading crown sometimes matches its height. And the trunk may be branch-free for 60'!

You'll never forget the sight of a huge sycamore tree. The trunk, haphazardly exposed in areas by peeling bark, looks eerily white. The upper branches usually entwine at angles. The large leaves—often 10" wide—have a shiny green top surface and a pale undersurface. By fall, sycamore's fruit shows up—fuzzy seed clusters called buttonballs.

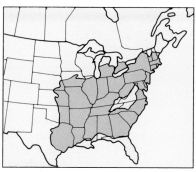

Natural range

Sycamore's coarse-grained wood has a pale reddish cast. Interwoven fibers give the wood hardness and elasticity, but at the same time, make it difficult to season when flat-sawed. Quarter-sawed sycamore displays an attractive fleck pattern in the grain. At about 35 pounds per cubic foot air dried, the wood matches cherry in weight.

Uses in woodworking

Manufacturers of boxes and crates use the largest share of sycamore because it is strong, has no odor, and imparts no taste. In the home workshop, properly seasoned sycamore shapes up as a tough utility wood for frames and cabinet carcasses. As unfinished drawer sides, the wood actually becomes smoother and slides easier *continued*

SYCAMORE
continued

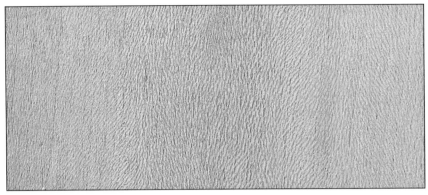

Plain-sawed sycamore

with use. And quarter-sawed, it can become attractive furniture. Its rayed grain also makes impressive turnings.

Availability

Large hardwood dealers catering to commercial accounts, and sawmills located within its range, will likely carry sycamore. To take advantage of grain pattern, much sycamore becomes veneer. Lumber should cost less than $1 per board foot, and veneer 30 cents per square foot.

Improper seasoning methods and an overly hasty kiln-drying schedule result in stained and warped sycamore. Processors familiar with this wood, though, produce uniformly colored, durable, stable stock. So, shop before you buy.

Machining methods

Sycamore reacts to machining or hand tools almost like cherry, but in some instances matches maple's annoying tendency to burn. *Any problems or unusual handling are noted in the following tips:*

• Sycamore planes and joints easily, but has a moderate blunting effect on cutting edges much like maple. Figured or quarter-sawed stock requires shallower cuts and a slow feed rate.

• Because sycamore lacks the stiffness of cherry, it isn't as likely to break out or chip in crosscutting. Ripping straight-grained stock poses no problems, even without carbide-tipped blades. Avoid tearout in quarter-sawed or figured wood by leaving enough for a jointing pass to clean the edge after sawing.

• Sycamore routes readily. Figured or quarter-sawed stock may burn more readily than plain stock, so maintain a consistent feed rate without forcing the bit through the wood.

• Drilling at medium speeds produces clean holes with no breakout. Lift the bit occasionally to clear debris. This technique avoids burning.

• Sycamore sands effortlessly to a glasslike finish, and, if left unfinished in a project, such as drawer parts, for example, it will actually burnish itself smooth.

• All adhesives work well on sycamore. And because the wood resists splitting, pilot holes aren't required, unless you seat screws by hand.

• Plain-sawed sycamore without figure stains well and accepts any finish. It's easily dyed to any color. Before staining figured or quarter-sawed wood, test the stain on

scrap for even penetration. A wood conditioner may be required in some cases to avoid blotchiness.

Carving comments

For unknown reasons sycamore rarely shows up in carvings, although it isn't as hard as cherry and can be carved with chisels and a mallet or power-carving tools as easily.

• The grain flecks caused by the wood's rays make it ideal for clear-finished sculptural subjects where they would add visual interest. However, they would detract from a detailed carving unless paint were used.

Turning tricks

Except for its slight tendency to dull tools, sycamore turns exceptionally well, producing smooth turnings that require little sanding. An excellent choice for between-centers work, such as spindles and balusters.

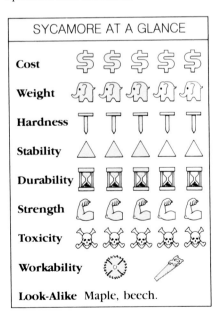

TEAK

The tropic's top seafaring stock

Sailors and traders visiting India and China in the early 1800s were caught up with the wood they found in widespread use as seagoing stock. Teak, with working and structural properties surpassing even those of their traditional oak, soon became the prime nautical wood of Europe and America. Weather-resistant, tough teak still ranks as the favorite for boat decks and trim. But, it's the story of how this hardwood arrives in craftsmen's hands that rivals its history.

Teak harvesting begins with the girdling of selected trees deep in a Southeast Asian rain forest. This allows the timbers to die and dry on the stump over a period of years, making them tons lighter at logging time. Because of the terrain and its remoteness, elephants play a major role, moving the massive logs miles to a river. There, the teak lies for months, awaiting monsoon rains to fill the banks so it can float from the interior. In

traditional forest harvesting, this seasonal reliance often results in a five-year delivery time.

Wood identification

Teak *(Tectona grandis),* a native species in the rain forests of Burma, India, Laos, and Thailand, now grows in about 40 countries throughout the tropics. In Java, for instance, teak was planted generations ago, and the trees are managed for sustained yield.

Naturally occurring teak grows to heights of 100' and diameters of 12' or more in about 300 years. Plantation-grown teak gets taller, but never as large in circumference, although it can be harvested in 60 years.

If size alone didn't distinguish teak from other rain forest trees, its enormous leaves would. They can measure a whopping 24×36", and their top surface is rough enough to sand with!

Teak has a thin layer of yellow sapwood, but it's never seen by woodworkers. Importers and dealers instead favor boards of only coarse-textured, golden-

Natural range

brown heartwood. Teak, though, depending on its growing conditions, may have a greenish tint, small stripes of yellow and darker colors, or an occasional mottle figure. At about 40 pounds per cubic foot dry, teak weighs slightly less than oak.

Silica, which the growing tree extracts from the ground and distributes throughout the wood, gives teak an oily feeling and causes finishing problems. Freshly sawed boards also carry the aroma of old shoe leather.

continued

TEAK
continued

Teak heartwood

Uses in woodworking

Because it defies the elements, teak makes the perfect candidate for garden furniture and outdoor structures. Indoors, teak always has been prime stock for clean-lined furniture, as well as all forms of cabinetry.

Cost and availability

The Burmese set the grading and pricing standard for teak over 100 years ago. That's why teak's price goes up with the width and length of the board. For instance, First European Quality teak boards 1" thick will be at least 8" wide and bring a premium of $10 or more per board foot. Narrower boards cost less.

Prime teak-faced plywood runs considerably more than red oak or cherry panels, but at around $85, falls below the cost of walnut. Veneer prices fall into the $1.50 per square foot range of most imported species.

Woodworkers with lots of experience working teak say that in old-growth trees from Thailand and Burma, the silica in the wood has broken down, making it easier to machine. However, younger, plantation-grown teak has practically the same performance qualities as old-growth and you'll

notice little difference in machining, although the color may vary, depending on the conditions at the location where it grew.

Machining methods

Because teak does vary in color according to its origin, try to buy all the boards you need for your project from the same shipment so the overall tone of your project will be uniform. *When working it, keep these tips in mind:*

• Due to its silica and oil content, teak slides easily over a machine's iron bed. You'll have no problem planing and jointing it, except that teak does dull blades more quickly than other hardwoods.

• In spite of its hardness, teak rips and crosscuts more easily than oak. Always use carbide blades.

• Teak poses no routing problems, but it quickly dulls bits.

• With proper woodworking drill bits and high speed, you can put clean holes in this wood without breakout.

• Sanding teak requires frequent stops to clear its sticky dust away with a stiff brush. *Caution:* Some people have an allergic reaction to teak dust.

• Epoxy or resorcinol adhesives work best when joining teak. But first scrub all wood to be joined with acetone, then let it dry.

• Finishing teak poses the most difficulty. The wood doesn't take stain exceptionally well, and traditional clear finishes (except lacquer) can be a problem. For instance, regular polyurethane won't set up. But two-part polyurethane, the type for marine use, will. That's why teak is frequently coated with a penetrating oil, such as tung or teak.

• For outdoor use, teak doesn't require a finish, only an occasional

scrubbing with soap and water to clean the surface. The wood will eventually weather to a pleasing gray color.

Carving comments

Teak ranks high in hardness, but you can carve it with chisels and a mallet.

• The wood takes fine detail. However, the silica in the wood dulls chisels in no time.

• Take shallow cuts, despite how easily the wood seems to slice away, or else your cutting edge may wander in the coarse grain.

• Power carvers should arm themselves with carbide cutting burrs to endure this wood.

Turning tricks

Except for its tendency to dull tools, teak turns exceptionally well in response to shearing cuts. Some teak, though, primarily from India, may be somewhat brittle and coarse-textured, causing chipping or splintering.

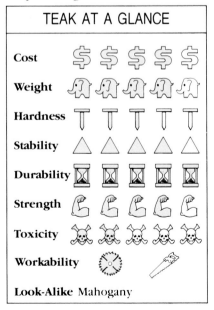

TEAK AT A GLANCE					
Cost	💲	💲	💲	💲	💲
Weight	🐘	🐘	🐘	🐘	🐘
Hardness	T	T	T	T	T
Stability	△	△	△	△	△
Durability	⧗	⧗	⧗	⧗	⧗
Strength	💪	💪	💪	💪	💪
Toxicity	☠	☠	☠	☠	☠
Workability	⚙			🪚	
Look-Alike Mahogany					

WESTERN RED CEDAR

The durable, decay-resistant tree of life

Botanist Louis Nee discovered western red cedar on Vancouver Island in the Pacific Northwest about 1794. Long before he ventured there, the region's Indians were making planked lodges of the lightweight, yet highly durable, wood. Outside, next to the lodges, stood towering, carved totems depicting family histories. Also made of western red cedar, many of the poles still stand near Ketchikan, in southeastern Alaska.

This versatile tree, once called giant *arborvitae,* the "tree of life," was exactly that to the coastal tribes. It provided them with long, tough strands of bark that they wove into baskets, braided for rope, and cast as fishing lines. For travel, they made 50'-long canoes of hollowed logs.

The first daring pioneers in that wild land soon learned to work western red cedar, too. Since then, the wood has been extensively used for outdoor construction, shingle and shake roofing, siding, boats, and just about any project demanding decay-resistance.

Wood identification

A tree of the cool, damp coastland, western red cedar *(Thuja plicata)* grows in moist soil from southern Alaska to northern California. The western slopes of the Rocky Mountains in Idaho, Montana, and British Columbia form the eastern limit of its range. On the rain-washed coast, the tree can reach heights of 190' and diameters of 10' or more.

Western red cedar may have as many names as branches. Some people call it canoe cedar, or shingle wood, while others refer to the tree as Lawson cypress and Pacific red cedar. Western red cedar's Latin name, though, loosely translates to "sweet-smelling wood with plaited leaves." And the characteristic smell as well as the leaves help you identify it. The flat, lacy-looking sprigs of small, braided leaves (not needles!) give off a spicy aroma, as does the wood. The thin reddish-brown bark resembles cinnamon in color, and comes off in strings.

Medium- to coarse-grained, western red cedar completely lacks pitch or resin. The small amount of sapwood you'll find is almost pure white. The heartwood varies from a dark, reddish brown to a pale yellow. With age, the color dulls to a silver-gray.

Working properties

Lightweight at about 28 pounds per cubic foot, western red cedar has low shock resistance. It's also

Western red cedar heartwood

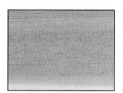

Western red cedar heartwood with sapwood

only moderately limber, but you can count on red cedar's stability.

Work this wood with both hand and power tools. Use caution, though, when planing or sanding so you won't catch and tear the grain. While western red cedar does not hold nails well, it glues easily.

For exterior use, western red cedar takes and holds paint and stain with persistence. Inside, finish it with lacquer, varnish, or clear wax.

Uses in woodworking

You can rely on western red cedar anywhere you want the warm color of wood, and durability. Outdoors, it's perfect for carefree, long-lived decks, fences, and furniture; indoors, for wall treatments, cabinets, and moldings and millwork. Because it's soft, it makes a good carving wood. Combat the brittleness with a sharp blade.

Cost and availability

Clear heart western red cedar, the best grade, costs about $2 per board foot. A-grade, which can include some knots as well as hints of white sapwood, sells for less.

You can find it in standard softwood dimensions, both rough-cut or surfaced, at most lumberyards from the Midwest to the Pacific. Cost of shipping limits its availability in the East.

WHITE OAK

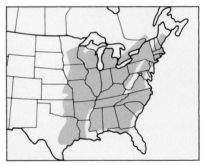

The weatherproof stock of Old Ironsides, barrels, and mission furniture

When England sought wood to rebuild her once-great naval fleet, eyes turned to the American colonies' forests of white oak because by the 1700s, English oaks had all been felled. British shipbuilders, though, scorned New World oak as inferior.

Proud American builders knew better, and built ships of native timber. The famed frigate *Constitution,* known as Old Ironsides, had a gun deck of Massachusetts white oak, a keel from New Jersey white oak, and frame and planks from magnificent Maryland trees.

As New England sea captains went on to sail their all-American, white-oak ships to the far corners of the world, another growing industry also made far-reaching use of the wood. Ever since colonial times, coopers had hand-riven staves of white oak for barrels. And as the young nation's merchant fleet increasingly sailed the seas, it carried with it more and more cooperage for export trade. Some of it was bound for France's vineyards, or to the West Indies for barreling rum and molasses.

Later, during the Victorian Age of the late 1800s, still another use emerged—as a fine furniture wood. Stained and highly varnished, it was sold as Golden Oak, and attained a popularity that persisted through the mission furniture of the 1920s. Today, even though somewhat revived for furniture and cabinets, white oak represents less than one fifth of all oak—red and white—harvested in the United States.

Wood identification

Although you can find dozens of species of white oak growing nearly everywhere in the U.S., the grandest of them all is *Quercus alba*. Called stave oak and forkleaf white oak, the tree can grow to ponderous size within its range. Trees more than 8' in diameter and over 150' tall have been recorded. Usually, the trees fall between a 3–4' diameter and an 80–100' height.

You can easily identify white oak by its round-lobed leaves (red-oak leaves have sharply pointed lobes). In the absence of leaves, check for white oak's telltale light, ash-gray bark with its scaly plates. Or, look for acorns. Those of the white oak have a shallow cap with an inside that's satiny smooth. The red-oak acorn cap is hairy inside.

Natural range

The wood of white oak isn't white as the name implies. It's tan. And unlike the end grain of red oak, which displays large open pores, that of white oak shows a tightly closed formation. Weighing about 47 pounds per cubic foot dry, white oak features a straight, coarse grain that when sawed on the quarter often produces a rippled figure.

Uses in woodworking

Unlike red oak, white oak resists moisture and decay, making it ideal for outdoor furniture and boats. Indoors, it's a cabinet-class wood for tables and chairs, floors and trim, and turnings. Basketmakers also rely on the green wood. But, due to its hardness, carvers aren't fond of it.

Flat-sawn white oak

Quarter-sawn white oak

Availability

The lumber industry lumps all white oaks together, so you may not always be getting *Quercus alba*. Don't worry, all species share the same wood traits.

Widely available at hardwood suppliers, white oak costs about $3 per board foot; triple that price for quarter-sawed wood. Veneer runs about 50 cents per square foot, and white-oak plywood is widely sold.

White oak requires careful handling during the drying process to ensure boards free from seasoning defects, such as internal honeycombing, so closely check any questionable boards before you buy. You also might inquire about the source of the wood. Slower-grown wood from the Appalachians and the north offers an easier-to-work texture than that from southern bottomlands, although they may look the same.

Machining methods

White oak's hardness requires power tools, but it shouldn't give you any problems as long as you keep the following in mind:

• Because white oak dulls cutting edges, use carbide-tipped cutters and saw blades.

• The wood's straight grain presents only moderate resis-

tance to ripping, but its hardness demands a slow feed rate.

• White oak also has a greater tendency to splinter than red oak. That means that you should take a few shallow passes on the planer or jointer when removing stock.

• When routing white oak, especially end grain, also take shallow passes. And be sure to use a backing board on cross-grain cuts for splinter- and chip-free machining.

• In counterboring, only quarter-sawed or rift-cut white oak presents a problem. The eye-appealing rays may lift or chip out, so work slowly. This hard wood also requires slower speeds (about 500 rpm or less) on the drill press.

• Again, the wood's hardness requires sanding with progressively finer grits. And don't attempt to orbit-sand this species because swirl marks are hard to remove.

• White oak's high tannic acid, when used for outdoor projects, will turn ordinary screws black and stain the wood. Although they cost more, use brass or stainless steel fasteners for long-lasting good looks. And always predrill white oak for fasteners.

• Don't use casein glue with white oak. Its components react with the high tannic acid content of the wood and the bond won't properly adhere.

• White oak responds to all stains and finishes well, and unlike open-grained red oak, there's no need to fill for smoothness.

Carving comments

Armed with a mallet and very sharp gouges (or power-carving tools), only determined carvers tackle white oak. One tip: Grind cutting edges to a deep bevel of 25°–30° for roughing in. For the shallower, shaving cuts of detail work, return to 15°–20° bevel.

Turning tricks

• For turning between centers, avoid splintering by entering the wood with a sharp, clean-cutting tool, such as a skew, and take shallow cuts.

• Sharpen your turning tools more frequently when working white oak so that they never abrade the wood.

WHITE OAK AT A GLANCE				
Cost	💲	💲	💲	💲 💲
Weight				
Hardness				
Stability	△	△	△	△ △
Durability				
Strength				
Toxicity				
Workability				
Look-Alike Red oak				

YELLOW BIRCH

The shimmering queen of the north

There's no sight in the woods that quite compares to a stand of yellow birch. The bronze-barked trees glisten against their neighbors. Light bounces off them, as if reflected from metal.

The beauty of yellow birch on the stump probably captivated colonial New England craftsmen, too. But, it was the tree's strong, golden wood that they treasured. From it, they expertly crafted Windsor-style chairs, tables, and other furniture to withstand decades of use and abuse. Centuries later—at the peak of this

wood's popularity in the 1950s—homes across the nation featured sturdy, blonde cabinets of yellow birch.

Wood identification

Yellow birch *(Betula alleghaniensis)*, also called silver birch and swamp birch, is one of 50 species of birch found around the world. Situated in a wide range across the northern U.S. and Canada, yellow birch grows best in rich, moist woodlands by rivers and streams.

Easily recognized by its metallic-looking bark with numerous papery curls and strips, the forest-grown yellow birch attains 60–70' heights and 3' diameters.

Before leaves appear in the spring, twigs bear brown buds and branch ends boast two or three catkins containing pollen. By summer, the buds develop into toothed and pointed leaves measuring about 3–4" long.

Along the branches, small cones with seeds inside appear, only to drop off in the fall.

What little sapwood you find in yellow birch will be nearly white, while heartwood has an array of color. The wood varies from cream to golden tan to light walnut. Some wood may even have gray and red tinges.

Natural range

Although birch has a distinct grain pattern—sometimes displaying waves or curls—the fine-textured wood doesn't always overpower the eye. And, at 43 pounds per cubic foot dry, it weighs almost the same as sugar maple, although it's not as hard.

Uses in woodworking

Along with maple, yellow birch has always been a standard for items that get lots of use—chairs, tables, desks, and cabinets. And, it often turns up as doors and moldings as well as floors.

Many of the turned products sold in home centers are yellow birch. It's also used for dowels dowel pins, screw-hole buttons and plugs, and shaker pegs.

Availability

Yellow birch lumber usually sells for about $2 per board foot, and,

Plain yellow birch

Curly yellow birch

except on the West Coast, should be readily available. Stock from the northern part of its range is harder, has fewer defects, and stains better.

Although you normally won't find lumber with much sapwood, manufacturers of rotary cut yellow birch veneer make the distinction. It's offered as "natural," including heartwood and sapwood, and "select white," from sapwood. Plywood sells for about $50 per sheet.

Machining methods

Yellow birch machines a little easier than maple, a wood with similar characteristics. That's because yellow birch normally has a finer, more even grain than maple. However, it does have a moderate dulling effect on cutting edges that requires carbide tips. *When yellow birch does misbehave, here's what to do:*

• The wood planes smoothly 90 percent of the time. However, spinning cutters, as on a planer, sometimes catch wavy grain and tear out a pockmark. When this occurs, try reversing the board and taking a shallower cut.

• Yellow birch normally joints cleanly, but trying to decide grain direction to determine feed sometimes can be impossible. When in doubt as to feed direction, set table

height for cuts of ⅟₁₆" to ⅛" and decide by trial and error

• Nearly as dense as maple, yellow birch requires ripping with a rip-profile blade of 24 teeth or fewer to avoid clogging. A steady feed rate reduces burning.

• In crosscutting, steel fine-toothed plywood blades work well to avoid splintering. Today's thinly veneered birch plywood splinters easily, too. Score the line to be cut or place masking tape on the kerf line and saw right through it.

• Back drill bits out frequently to clear the hole and avoid burning, especially in end grain.

• Use router bits with ballbearing pilots to avoid burning, and, if possible, rout slowly. Cross-grain cuts require shallow passes.

• Beware of squeeze-out when gluing. Dry glue, when scraped off, can grab the wood and tear it away. To detect squeeze-out, wipe the wood with paint thinner. And, don't let clamps contact squeeze-out—black stains result.

• Wipe yellow birch with a damp cloth to raise grain prior to staining or clear-finishing. Sand, then stain. When grain has a differing color or pattern, expect uneven staining, or first prepare the surface with a product such as Minwax Wood Conditioner.

Carving comments

• Yellow birch, although hard, does take fine detail and has its place in relief work. It requires special handling, however.

• Gouge bevels (15° to 20°) dull quickly. Keep a sharp edge with a 10° bevel on the *back side*.

• Wavy grain will be more difficult to carve because the wavy areas will be harder than the plain.

• Power carvers should not begin with coarse-cutting burrs—the wood splinters. Use medium-cut burrs, then follow with finer ones.

Turning tips

Yellow birch couldn't be easier to turn with sharp tools, aside from these exceptions:

• Scraping can produce splinters.

• Sanding the wood on the lathe across grain produces scratches. Instead, wipe with a damp cloth, then stop the lathe and sand with the grain using fine paper.

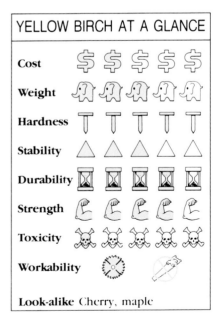

YELLOW BIRCH AT A GLANCE	
Cost	$ $ $ $ $
Weight	🐘 🐘 🐘 🐘 🐘
Hardness	⊤ ⊤ ⊤ ⊤ ⊤
Stability	△ △ △ △ △
Durability	⧖ ⧖ ⧖ ⧖ ⧖
Strength	💪 💪 💪 💪 💪
Toxicity	☠ ☠ ☠ ☠ ☠
Workability	🪚 🪚
Look-alike Cherry, maple	

ACKNOWLEDGMENTS

Writers

Bill Krier with Jim Boelling and Jim Downing—Ten Winning Ways to Work With Plywood, pages 36–41

Larry Clayton—How to Transform Found Wood into Usable Stock, pages 28–31

Peter J. Stephano—How to Be a Hardwood Sleuth, pages 13–15; What You Should Know About Toxic Wood, pages 21–24; How to Succeed at Air-Drying Lumber, pages 42–43

Carl Voss—Pressure-Treated Wood, pages 18–20

Photographers

California Redwood Assn.
Bob Calmer
W.A. Côté, S.U.N.Y., Syracuse
John Hetherington
Hopkins Associates
William Hopkins
Jim Kascoutas
Marlen Kemmet
Bob Laramie
Scott Little
N.C. Brown Center for Ultrastructure Studies
Tom Wegner
Western Wood Product Assn.
Gary Zeff

Illustrators

Kim Downing
Mike Henry
Brian Jensen
Steve Schindler
Jim Stevenson

If you would like to order any additional copies of our books, call 1-800-678-2802 or check with your local bookstore.